Preface

Northwood continues to update its texts to retain relevancy and to be in the mainstream of the real world. As the leading university in Automotive Marketing worldwide, we are indeed proud to continue the discipline created in the mid 1960s, when the curriculum began with the advertisement and cooperation of the National Automobile Dealers Association. This revised text, Dealership Business Management, is one of a series of texts prepared for management students in Automotive Marketing at Northwood and for personnel in the automotive industry.

Our thanks to the Domestic and Automobile Manufacturers and their Divisions and Dealers and to the Import Distributors and their Dealers, for the basic research information which preceded this edition. Our text rewriting research expenses are funded primarily by regular contributions from member associations of the Automotive Trade Association Executives (ATAE). Additional content support was provided by Reynolds & Reynolds and Universal Underwriters. We thank them all.

Northwood has been the educational source for thousands of automotive students for over a quarter century. Our graduates are beginning to swell the ranks of dealership principals and manufacturers/distributors. Thousands of others have had varied degrees of training through the auspices of Northwood. Their records of achievement reflect our institutional commitment to the free enterprise system and the private sector wherein our futures lies.

Dr. David E. Fry
President
Northwood University
October 1995

CONTENTS

CHAPTER 1

CHAPTER I

INTRODUCTION TO BUSINESS MANAGEMENT

Dealership Business Management Defined

Management is traditionally defined by its functions. In fact, the most generally accepted definitions involve a list of functions that state good management exists when these listed functions are coordinated to reach a given objective. This is like saying an airplane consists of wings, a motor, and various other components, and successfully meets its objective when it lands safely at its destination.

Dealership Business Management as a part of the management discipline is almost exclusively related to profit, or return on investment in an existing or planned dealership. Return on investment (ROI) is probably a Dealers key concern.

$$ROI = \frac{\text{Net Profit Before Taxes}}{\text{Initial Investment} + \text{Retained Earnings}}$$

It may seem simplistic, but 100 units at $600 gross gives the same return as 1000 units at $60. This relationship is often given as one of the fundamental conflicts between manufacturers and Dealers, and is used in arguments relative to Dealer concentration. This Dealer concern limits our consideration to the control function, i.e., is the dealership earning a satisfactory return and is each segment (department) contributing its share? The analysis generally involves:

- Investigating information affecting sales and gross profit
- Making a decision as to whether performance is or is not adequate
- Determining if additional analysis is needed, or if corrective action is required

For the purposes of this text, Dealership Business Management is defined as the control of dealership activities to insure they fall within acceptable guidelines. In most instances we will be dealing with history that has been reduced to numerical relationships. However, the actual business decisions must be made in light of present and future market conditions. The reader is thus reminded that the successful entrepreneur uses business management as a <u>tool</u> and an <u>essential element</u> in the decision-making process. Because of prospective customer's perceptions, the decision to price a unit at $16,000 or $16,500, is really more art than science.

Implicit in our definition is the concept of **efficiency** ordinarily expressed by **lowest cost**. **Efficiency** and **cost** can be elusive concepts. For example, a decision to lower our costs today by canceling our garage liability policy could increase costs if later we incurred an insurable loss. For that reason, the first section of this book deals exclusively with **analyzing financial** information with the remainder of the text discussing items such as **insurance** and **personnel** that must be considered in business decisions.

Basic Accounting Concepts

The Business Manager in the automobile dealership is not <u>always</u> a professional accountant. However, in today's multiple-dealership operations, the Business Manager is usually a professional accountant or even a Certified Public Accountant. In those dealerships where the manager is not an accountant, he or she still must understand general accounting practices and procedures in the dealership, since it is his or her responsibility to compile the evidence of progress, or lack of progress, in every department of the dealership.

Accounting and **Bookkeeping** often are used interchangeably as terms. Furthermore, the keeping of books and records is so much a part of accounting that the dividing line between the two seems, at times, to be virtually non-existent. The difference becomes defined, however, if bookkeeping is regarded as the routine, record-keeping aspect of accounting. Accounting, on the other hand, combines analysis and interpretation with the keeping of records.

In an automobile dealership, analysis and interpretation based upon accurate and complete records is vital to the financial well-being of the business. Thus, the Business Manager, in assuming the role of accountant for his dealership, serves as the dealership's financial guardian.

The importance of maintaining all accounting records so that they reflect a true financial condition of the dealership <u>cannot be too strongly emphasized</u>. Under no other circumstances can correct conclusions be drawn and proper corrective action taken unless accounting records are well maintained. When accounting records are inaccurate or incomplete, the inevitable results are errors in judgment and poor management decisions. Indeed, the majority of business failures are often the result of inaccurate accounting. Sound accounting procedures, then, are essential to good management.

An introduction to accounting follows:

Assets = Liabilities + Net Worth

Assets: Are those items used in conducting business. Typical assets would include land and facilities, if owned, note receivables, equipment, inventories and furnishings.

Liabilities: Are claims against a business by outsiders. Common liabilities include notes payables and long-term debt.

Net Worth: The net worth, or owner's equity, is the difference between assets owned and liabilities owed to outsiders.

Assets are used in conducting the dealership business. The sum of the assets employed in the business must equal the sum of the rights to the assets. These rights or claims on assets are called equities. Equities represent claims against the assets by the owner and creditors. The equity of the owners is called net worth. The equities of outsiders are called liabilities.

In order to manage a business efficiently, the financial condition of the business must be known periodically. Creditors, stockholders and the government also desire financial information. The balance sheet is an accounting summary that presents the financial status of a business on a given date; it is a snapshot of the financial condition of a business. The specific needs of the business determine if the balance sheet is to be constructed annually, quarterly, or monthly. Dealerships generally prepare monthly balance sheets. Often called the statement of financial condition, the balance sheet is an expansion of the basic accounting equation: Assets = Liabilities + Net Worth.

The account and the report balance sheet forms are both an expansion of the basic accounting equation. In the report form, the liabilities and net worth are listed below the total of the assets. In the account form, the assets are listed on the left, liabilities and net worth on the right.

While the balance sheets of small businesses are relatively simple, the balance sheets of larger businesses are obviously more complex. Statement construction requires that similar financial items be classified and listed in a logical, systematic order. Pertinent information relative to the items should also be included. The detail presented depends primarily upon who is to use the statement. Of course, management might be vitally interested in operating facts that would be of little concern to creditors or stockholders. Automobile manufacturers have specific financial statements that they require their Dealers to complete. Additionally, they have their own sets of accounting standards that must also be followed, including the completion of the financial statement by the tenth day of the following month.

A better understanding of the basic principles of statement construction and their relationship to the accounting equation is gained by examining the example statement. The name of the business, the type of statement, and the date are told by the heading. The date, if omitted, leaves the reader without a basis for comparison. Comparisons related to past periods or business averages determine how well the Dealership is doing. The major sections, classifications, and items in order of their appearance on the balance sheet are discussed in the following paragraphs.

ASSETS

The asset section is the first part of the accounting equation. Assets (items of value owned by the business) are classified into three groups: current assets, fixed assets and other assets.

Current Assets

Current assets are those assets that can be converted into cash within a twelve-month operating cycle. Prepaid expenses such as payroll or taxes are included, for if not paid in advance, cash would ultimately be reduced by the same amount in the near future. The items within the current asset classification are usually listed in the order of their liquidity or the ease with which an item may be converted into cash. Current assets include cash, notes receivable, accounts receivable, inventories and prepaid expenses, plus many others.

The **cash** in a business may be **on hand**, **on deposit in the bank**, or as **contracts in transit**, which are the amounts due from finance institutions on customer notes discounted (finance contracts executed by the dealership at the time of the new or used vehicle sale).

Notes Receivable are claims of the dealership against outsiders in the form of promissory notes, time drafts and trade acceptances. These items can be negotiable and must meet requirements prescribed by law. They are readily converted into cash by discounting or are given in payment of obligations by negotiation.

Accounts Receivable are claims against other businesses or persons which customarily arise from the sale of merchandise. The Account Receivable is the business's or person's promise to pay. Account receivable balances generally result from parts, service or body shop sales, and rarely are affected by new or used car sales. Although it may vary, most receivable accounts are basically charge accounts opened by area businesses who service their vehicles at the dealership.

The Factory Receivables - Other account includes funds due from the manufacturer for new vehicle consumer incentives. **The amounts owed the dealership for these incentive activities can be substantial.** If left without close supervision, they can significantly increase the receivables account and have a _**huge**_ impact on the dealership's cash flow position. This account should be monitored daily, particularly during times of high manufacturer-sponsored consumer incentive activity. Questions to ask include: Are incentive claims reported within 24 hours of the affected delivery? Are the proper incentive codes applied during the delivery reporting process? Are rejects followed up by the business manager until they are resolved?

The new car, used car, parts and accessories inventories represent merchandise intended for resale. Historically, they were carried on the statement at book value after any LIFO write-downs. The total value of each inventory may be determined by Physical count or by book inventory. All parts and vehicle inventories are carefully audited by physical count or inspection. Due to their high inventory cost, vehicle inventories are usually counted/inspected once each month. Parts physical inventory counts are typically conducted once each year.

Insurance premiums paid in advance and unused are reported as an asset. Similarly, items used in the office such as repair orders, pencils, computer paper, machine tapes, etc., are consumed in the operation of the business. Assets purchased in advance and unused appear as assets on the balance sheet in the form of prepaid expense. When these items are used, the asset account is diminished and the expense is recorded. It would be far too labor intensive and unproductive to account for every single supply item by actual cost. Therefore, the Business Manager will estimate what the consumed supplies are or will simply utilize invoice receipts from supply purchases.

Fixed Assets

In the automobile business, fixed assets are those which are relatively permanent or fixed. They are characterized by large cost, and used throughout their lives. Their gradual decrease in value is expressed in accounting as depreciation. When no longer useful, they are scrapped or sold. Examples of fixed assets are land, buildings, machinery and shop equipment, and furniture and fixtures.

In the dealership, much operating equipment is necessary. The book value of hoists, power tools, diagnostic equipment, uni-body frame machines, paint booths, and many other necessary assets are reported in this group.

The book value of office and salesroom furniture and fixtures includes such items as tables, desks, chairs, calculators, computers, display equipment and furnishings.

If the land being used by the business is owned, the cost of the land appears on the statement as an asset. Fixed assets generally depreciate through use in the business over a long period of time. Land is the exception. In business operations, land does not deteriorate. Since land and buildings are frequently purchased for a lump sum, the accountant arrives at a separate cost for each. Only the cost of the building is considered in determining depreciation.

The cost of the building(s) is on the balance sheet as an asset. If the business rents the premises, as many dealerships do, the building is not owned and does not appear on the statement.

LIFO

Special care must be used in considering inventory value if LIFO (Last in, first out) is used. Every dealership should consult with a CPA who has expertise in this area. It is particularly important because IRS regulations do change, potentially having serious impact on the dealership.

Basically, LIFO is a legal method of cost accounting that permits the accountant to use the last cost of purchase for the cost of all previous sales. For example, if the cost of a car purchased on December 1 included a price increase of $300, then that increased cost could be used for all cars sold in the previous months. LIFO understates profit, which permits a lower income tax liability for a current year. This increases cash flow. The amount of the understated profit is carried as a LIFO reserve which may be payable at a future date if there is a deflation.

Other Assets

There are other, nonfranchise assets, i.e., those not used in the automobile business. Examples include real estate, loans to outsiders and investments in affiliated enterprises.

Items shown under this heading are not related to the normal course of business activity. Traditionally, the concern has been transferred to other investments. In today's world of tight credit and high interest rates, items can be included because of additional security demanded by the financing institution.

LIABILITIES

Liabilities are classified into two main groups: Current liabilities and long term debt.

Current Liabilities

Those liabilities that will be due and payable within one year from the date of the balance sheet are termed **Current Liabilities**. The purchase of parts from a factory on 30-day open account represents a current-maturing liability. Normally, the potential ability of the business to pay current liabilities is found in the current assets. Current liabilities are primarily **accounts payable**, **notes payable** and **accrued liabilities**.

Depending upon the terms granted by the creditor, the purchase of parts, accessories and operating supplies may be made on open account for thirty or possibly sixty days. Quite common with automobile manufacturers is the establishment of the Open Parts Account. This account is used to track all costs for parts the dealership orders, and for charges for other products or services that might be supplied to the Dealer. Examples of these include training expenses, satellite link-up charges, Dealer communications, incentive programs for sales or service personnel and others. These accounts are also used to serve as a way for the manufacturer to reimburse the Dealer for items such as floor plan credits, holdback and others. In those cases, the account is credited and sometimes results in a credit balance. More common is the debit balance, which most manufacturers require payment by the tenth day of the following month.

Accounts Payables represent an obligation to pay the net balances due trade and other creditors within the granted credit period.

Notes Payables are instruments given by the business in payment of an amount owed to finance institutions. Promissory notes and trade acceptances may be given in payment of inventory purchases. In the automobile business, the financing by the Dealer of new vehicles purchased with a note secured by new cars in inventory is called **Floor Planning**. Floor Planning is almost always the most significant liability a dealership carries, as well as cost. The inventory may be floor planned through the manufacturers' finance division or through a local bank. Generally, the interest cost of floor planning ranges between .75 to 1.25 % over the current prime lending rate. Needless to say, sound expense controls over new car inventories are crucial to the dealership's overall ability to make a profit.

Two examples of **Accrued Liabilities** are payroll and taxes. At the time of statement preparation, the business may owe employees for services, but payment is not made. The accountant includes these amounts in the current liabilities for a truer picture of liabilities. Due to the methods used by the government in the collection of taxes, certain sales taxes, real estate taxes, payroll taxes and income taxes may be owed but not due. The accountant reflects these amounts as liabilities on the statement.

Long-Term Debt

These liabilities consist of large obligations that will not be due and payable within a year. The most common form of long-term liability results from the purchase of the dealership and/or its facilities and property. It may also include loans for major renovations to the facilities. If the method of retiring the liability requires installment payments, the portion of the balance falling due within a year appears in the current liabilities section.

Net Worth

The net worth section of the statement presents the owner's equity in the business as of the date of the balance sheet. It also shows changes that have taken place in the owner's equity since the date of the last statement. Therefore, the section first shows the previous equity and, following that, the effect on net worth resulting from profits, withdrawals and additional investments made since the last statement. Net worth is always equal to total assets less total liabilities. (Net Worth = Assets - Liabilities)

Recording Transactions

The accountant records the increases and decreases in accounts (accounts are business items and activities on which a continued record is maintained for operating information). The most simple account ("T" account) shows the name of the account and the monetary increases and decreases that have taken place. More detailed accounts show transaction dates and explanations after each transaction. The account seen below is a "T" account because it resembles the letter "T".

Title

Debit	Credit

This type of account is impractical, as it provides limited information. However, because of its simplicity, T-accounts will be used for illustrative purposes.

DEBITS AND CREDITS

Fr. John Goodrow's article "Accounting," (Daily Times News, 8 March 1971, Mt. Pleasant, Michigan), relates that, "In the 13th century Italian merchants began to keep track of their business affairs by making two entries, one of debit and one of credit. Essential to this innovation was...awareness of companies as continuing enterprises. However, each transaction was viewed separately, and the concept of "balance" in a Ledger was unknown. No attempt had been made to learn if a business was operating profitably over a specified period of time...It was (Franciscan Friar Lucas) Pacioli's contribution to record and classify the necessary elements of a balance sheet in...his "summa arithmetica"...in the year 1494.

Due to the complexity of modern business transactions, the original meaning and use of the words debit and credit have little significance. Sometimes the word "charge" is used for "debit." However, through years of use, the words debit and credit are today's accounting terminology.

A debit column and a credit column are provided in all accounts. In Latin, debit means "he owes" and credit means "he trusts". These ancient concepts were used when accounting records were kept primarily for transactions involving debtor and creditor relationships. Today you only have to remember debits are on the left side, credits are on the right side of "T" accounts.

The system of recording business transactions through the use of debits and credits is called double entry bookkeeping. It is acknowledged that Pacioli gave the world this system. Each business transaction must be analyzed into debits and credits, and the figures placed in the appropriate accounts. The expression, "the books are in balance," means that the sum of the debits recorded is equal to that of the credits.

The basic rules for debit and credit procedure in the recording of transactions are well established and uniformly used by accountants. The rules must be learned and their application **thoroughly** understood. The rules of the basic accounting equation are:

Debit:
Increase in asset accounts
Decreases in liability accounts
Decreases in net worth accounts

Credit:
Decreases in asset accounts
Increases in liability accounts
Increases in net worth accounts

The above rules are better understood when shown in diagram form as follows:

Assets	=	Liabilities + Net Worth
Increase with a debit		Increase with a credit
Decrease with a credit		Decrease with a debit

To apply the rules of debit and credit, the accountant must initially determine the financial items involved and classify them into assets, liabilities and net worth. Proper classification is vital if the correct rule is to be used. After classification, the increases and decreases in the account are recorded according to the rules of debit and credit.

Sales accounts increase Net Worth so these accounts are normally credits. Expense accounts decrease Net Worth so these accounts are normally debited. Liabilities are claims on assets by outsiders. Net Worth is the claim on assets by the owners (owner's equity).

Determining Account Balances

The balance of a T-account is found by totaling the debits and credits. The difference between the debits and credits is the balance. If the debits exceed the credits, the account has a debit balance. If the reverse is true, credits exceed debits, the account has a credit balance.

The general ledger is the book of final entry where transactions are summarized from journals and recorded in account form. In business, separate pages for general ledger accounts often are kept in computer printouts or loose-leaf binders. The accounts are usually arranged in order shown on the financial statement.

The trial balance of the general ledger consists of a listing and totaling of the debit and credit balances in order to prove the equality of debits and credits in the ledger. The trial balance proves that, in recording the transactions, total debits equal total credits. In addition, it proves that the arithmetical computation of the account balances is correct.

The Relationship between Accounting and Business Management

Business management consists of two very distinct but related functions: the accounting function and the business management function.

The accounting function, by itself, offers little in merchandising value; however, the business management function can be highly effective in the promotion of sales and the making of profits, provided its policies and procedures are sound and properly carried out. Nevertheless, this latter function cannot be performed without the facts produced by the former -- both are important to the dealership.

The business management function begins where the accounting function ends. Facts shown on the financial statement are the starting point of business management. Through an **analysis** of these data, it is possible to determine any out-of-line conditions. It's important to understand that a particular department may be operating profitably, but might still be considered out-of-line because it is not performing as well as perhaps it should be. Therefore out-of-line does not necessarily mean operating at a loss. An out-of-line condition might also be a single expense item listed on the profit and loss statement.

To reiterate, the dealership business manager is especially valuable to both the Dealer and the factory representative in their **interpretation of the accounting records as reflected on the financial statement**. It is the best tool for guidance of the dealership under all phases of the operation. Supplementary forms are important as aides for sales and profit management. There are also many comparative analysis tools made available through the manufacturer, NADA or Dealer 20 Groups.

The main objectives of the business management function can be defined as: (1) satisfactory profit, (2) volume of sales, (3) control of expenses, (4) ample liquid capital and (5) permanency. The reason a Dealer is in business is to make a profit. Business management is essential when selling goods in volume. The more the dealership sells, the more net profit it makes, providing that acceptable gross profits levels are maintained and expenses are controlled in line with the gross profit from those sales.

A Dealer requires adequate liquid capital to take full advantage of all selling opportunities. Not having liquid capital available for parts inventory, used car inventory, or for special promotions limits the dealership's ability to capitalize on promotional opportunities.

In the practice of business management, the Dealer takes three distinct steps: (1) Establishment of objectives, (2) monthly analysis of operations and (3) correction of out-of-line conditions.

First, the Dealer establishes objectives, most commonly known as a business plan or forecast. It is too late to manage anything after it has happened. Forecasts are required in all situations in which a current choice or decision has future implications. Good decision making can become better or worse, depending on the quality of the forecasts which become the basis for the decision making process.

Objectives are determined periodically by the Dealer, with the assistance of the department heads and especially the business manager. The factory representative is sometimes counseled. Objectives serve as operating guides and a performance evaluation base. They are the targets for the maximum number of sales within the potential market, and are to be accomplished by management actions and expenditures. Performance against past objectives is included in this analysis.

It is extremely important to set realistic objectives or forecasts. During the forecast process, the Dealer and Business Manager, along with other departmental managers must look at past performance, existing and anticipated local, regional and national economic forecasts. They must also look at issues such as what new fast-selling models are being introduced and their availability, discontinued products that may have previously sold well, a competitor entering or leaving the market and other local influences. Setting a 10% increase in gross new vehicle sales in an economy that is forecasted to be poor may not be realistic.

If progress against past objectives is not met, considering all other influential factors, there should be an analysis of the past actions taken in order to determine why the out-of-line conditions were not improved. This is accomplished by discussions with the department managers on a one-to-one basis.

The third step in the business management function is the correction of out-of-line conditions disclosed by the monthly analysis of the Dealer's financial statement. It would be poor judgment to assume that the plans to correct out-of-line conditions and to assign responsibility for their accomplishment were achieved. In fact, correcting out-of-line conditions requires the assignment of responsibility to specific individuals (usually Department Managers). Further, the individuals assigned the responsibility must be able to follow the progress on a daily, weekly or monthly basis, depending on the severity of the out-of-line condition.

CHAPTER 2

CHAPTER II

INTRODUCTION TO DEALERSHIP ACCOUNTING

Accounting Concepts Applied

It is pertinent to note, before proceeding, that dealership financial statements are basically the same. What differences exist between the statements recommended by manufacturers are generally minor in character; they all must present the same information.

It is the business manager's responsibility to furnish and make understandable the information requested by management, and to stay within the framework of the appropriate accounting policy manual and chart of accounts.

Failure to adhere to the approved system could result in unacceptable deviations from standards and norms, and make comparisons with Dealer composites or industry averages meaningless.

The more you are familiar with the accounting function, the easier it will be to grasp a particular system. A large number of Dealers have multiple franchises, and many readers will be in a position in the future of coordinating the progress of several franchises themselves.

The following examples apply the principles discussed in the previous chapter to dealership activities, and the end result shown on a representative balance sheet.

Transaction: David Ashby established a corporation with $1,000,000 stock issued and paid for.

    Debit: Cash $1,000,000

    Credit: Capital Stock $1,000,000

BALANCE SHEET

Assets		Liabilities	
Cash	$1,000,000	Net Worth	
		Capital Stock	$1,000,000
Total Assets	$1,000,000	Total Liabilities	
		and Net Worth	$1,000,000

DEALER
FINANCIAL STATEMENT

Dealer #: _____________
Region/Distrib.: _____________
Sales District #: _____________

COVERING PERIOD FROM _____________ THRU _____________ DEALER _____________

MAKES OTHER THAN MAZDA _____________ CITY _____________ STATE _____________

ASSETS

ASSETS	ACCT. NO.	AMOUNT	LINE NO.
CURRENT ASSETS			1
CASH			2
In Bank and on Hand	1000–1003	1 000 000	3
Contracts in Transit	1020		4
TOTAL CASH & CONTRACTS (LINES 3 TO 4 INCL.)		1 000 000	5
RECEIVABLES (MEMO PAST DUE — OVER 30 DAYS)			6
Vehicle Accounts	1110		7
Service, Parts & Body Shop	1120		8
Other Customer Accounts	1130		9
TOTAL CUSTOMER RECEIVABLES (LINES 7 TO 9 INCL.)			10
LESS: Allowance for Doubtful Accounts	1180		11
NET CUSTOMER RECEIVABLES (LINE 10 LESS 11)			12
Finance & Insurance Co. Receivables	1135		13
Other Factory Receivables	1136		14
Factory Receivables Incentive	1137		15
Warranty Claims Receivables-Mazda	1140		16
Warranty Claims Receivables-Other	1141		17
Transportation Claims Receivable	1150		18
Pre-Delivery Inspection	1180		19
TOTAL RECEIVABLES (LINES 12, 13 THRU 19 INCL.)			20
INVENTORIES (CARS / TRUCKS)			21
Demonstrators-Mazda (X)	1200		22
Demonstrators-Other (X)	1210		23
New Mazda (X)	1220		24
New Other (X)	1230		25
SUB TOTAL NEW & DEMO INVENTORY (LINES 22 THRU 25 INCL.)			26
LIFO Reserve-New Vehicles	1235		27
NET NEW & DEMO INVENTORY (LINE 26 LESS 27)			28
Used Vehicles ( )	1240		29
Memo OVER 30 DAYS ( )			30
Parts & Accessories-Mazda	1250		31
Parts & Accessories-Other	1260		32
SUB TOTAL PARTS & ACCESSORIES (LINES 31 & 32)			33
LIFO Reserve-Parts & Accessories	1265		34
NET PARTS & ACCESSORIES (LINE 33 LESS 34)			35
Gas, Oil & Grease	1270		36
Paint & Body Shop Materials	1272		37
Sublet Repairs	1275		38
Work in Process-Labor	1277		39
Miscellaneous Inventories	1280		40
TOTAL INVENTORIES (LINES 28, 29, 35 TO 40)			41
OTHER CURRENT ASSETS			42
Securities	1300		43
Prepaid Expense	1350		44
TOTAL OTHER CURRENT ASSETS (LINES 43 TO 44)			45
TOTAL CURRENT ASSETS (LINES 5, 20, 41 & 45)		1 000 000	46
Lease and Rental Units ( )	1400/1401		47
L & R ACCUMULATED WRITE DOWN	1421		48

FIXED ASSETS-AUTO BUSINESS ONLY

	ACCT. NO.	COST	ACCUMULATED DEPRECIATION	
LAND	1400			
BLDGS. & IMPROV.	1410 / 1411			
M & E EQUIP.	1440 / 1441			
P & A EQUIP.	1420 / 1422			
FURN. & FIXT.	1430 / 1435			
SERVICE UNITS	1450 / 1455			
LEASE-HOLDS	1460 / 1461			
360HV	1460 / 1475			
TOTAL (LINES 52 TO 59 INCL.)				
Memo.-Service Units: Cars (X) Trucks				

OTHER ASSETS

OTHER ASSETS	ACCT. NO.	AMOUNT	
Deposits	1600		63
Life Insurance-Cash Value	1620		64
Notes and Accounts Receivable-Officers	1630		65
Advances to Employees	1640		66
Other Assets & Investments	1650		67
Other Notes & Accounts Receivable	1670		68
TOTAL OTHER ASSETS (LINES 63 TO 68 INCL.)			69
TOTAL ASSETS (LINES 46, 47, 48, 60 & 69)		1 000 000	70

FORM MAZ-630-A1 (1PH) 1/84
Reynolds + Reynolds   1-800-344-0000

LIABILITIES

LINE NO.	LIABILITIES	ACCT. NO.	AMOUNT
1	**CURRENT LIABILITIES**		
2	**ACCOUNTS PAYABLE**		
3	Vendors	2000	
4	Customers Deposits	2005	
5	Other	2010	
6	TOTAL ACCOUNTS PAYABLE (LINES 3 TO 5 INCL.)		
7	**NOTES PAYABLE**		
8	New Vehicles & Demonstrators	2100	
9	Used Vehicles	2110	
10	Other	2115	
11	Current Amount-Long Term Debt	2117	
12	TOTAL NOTES PAYABLE (LINES 8 TO 11 INCL.)		
13	**ACCRUED LIABILITIES**		
14	Interest	2120	
15	Payroll	2130	
16	Insurance	2140	
17	Taxes-Payroll	2150	
18	Taxes-Sales	2160	
19	Taxes-Other	2170	
20	Income Taxes-Prior Year	2175	
21	Income Taxes-Current Year	2177	
22	Bonuses-Employees	2180	
23	Bonuses-Owners	2185	
24	Pension Fund	2190	
25	Other	2195	
26	Reserve for Repossession Losses	2199	
27	TOTAL ACCRUED LIABILITIES (LINES 14 TO 26 INCL.)		
28	TOTAL CURRENT LIABILITIES (LINES 6, 12 AND 27)		
29	**LONG TERM DEBT**		
30	Long Term Debt	2300	
31	Mortgages Payable-Real Estate	2310	
32	Lease & Rental Vehicles	2320	
33	Notes-Officers/Owners	2330	
34	TOTAL LONG TERM DEBT (LINES 30 TO 33)		
35	TOTAL LIABILITIES (LINES 28 & 34)		
36	**NET WORKING CAPITAL** $ _______ (ASSETS LINE 46 MINUS LIABILITIES LINE 28)		
37			
38			
39	**NET WORTH**		
40	**CORPORATION ONLY**		
41	PREFERRED STOCK	2800	
42	COMMON STOCK	2801	1 000 000
43	TREASURY STOCK	2802 ( )	
44	ADDITIONAL PAID IN CAPITAL	2805	
45	RETAINED EARNINGS	2810	
46	DIVIDENDS	2820 ( )	
47	**PROPRIETOR OR PARTNER**		
48	INVESTMENTS (LIST EACH PARTNER)	2830	
49			
50	DRAWINGS (LIST EACH PARTNER)	2840 ( )	
51			

MEMO: LIFO New Veh. / LIFO Parts / Total LIFO Res.

LINE		NEW		USED		PROFIT OR (LOSS) BEFORE TAXES (PG. 2 L-60-MONTH)
		MAZDA	OTHER	RETAIL	WHOLESALE	
52						
53	JAN					
54	FEB					
55	MAR					
56	APR					
57	MAY					
58	JUN					
59	JUL					
60	AUG					
61	SEP					
62	OCT					
63	NOV					
64	DEC					
65					— TOTAL UNITS	
66	PROFIT OR (LOSS) BEFORE TAXES (PAGE 2, LINE 60 MTH)					
67	ESTIMATED INCOME TAX (PAGE 2, LINE 62 YTD)					
68	NET PROFIT OR (LOSS) AFTER TAXES	2850				
69	TOTAL NET WORTH (LINES 40 TO 68 INCL.)			1 000 000		
70	TOTAL LIABILITIES & NET WORTH (LINES 35 & 69)			1 000 000		

OMIT CENTS

Transaction: Dealership leased facilities, prepaid three months rent at $10,000 per month.

    Debit: Prepaid Rent $30,000

    Credit: Cash $30,000

BALANCE SHEET

Assets		Liabilities	
Cash..$970,000		Net Worth	
Prepaid Rent...............................$ 30,000		Capital Stock...........................$1,000,000	
Total Assets..............................$1,000,000		Total Liabilities and net Worth.........................$1,000,000	

DEALER
FINANCIAL STATEMENT

Dealer # _______________

Region/Distrib. _______________

Sales District # _______________

COVERING PERIOD FROM ___________ THRU ___________ DEALER ___________

MAKES OTHER THAN MAZDA ___________ CITY ___________ STATE ___________

ASSETS	ACCT. NO.	AMOUNT	LINE NO.	LIABILITIES	ACCT. NO.	AMOUNT
CURRENT ASSETS			1	**CURRENT LIABILITIES**		
CASH			2	**ACCOUNTS PAYABLE**		
In Bank and on Hand	1000-1003	970 000	3	Vendors	2000	
Contracts in Transit	1020		4	Customers Deposits	2005	
TOTAL CASH & CONTRACTS (LINES 3 TO 4 INCL.)		970 000	5	Other	2010	
RECEIVABLES MEMO PART DUE-OVER 30 DAYS			6	TOTAL ACCOUNTS PAYABLE (LINES 3 TO 5 INCL.)		
Vehicle Accounts	1110		7	**NOTES PAYABLE**		
Service, Parts & Body Shop	1120		8	New Vehicles & Demonstrators	2100	
Other Customer Accounts	1130		9	Used Vehicles	2110	
TOTAL CUSTOMER RECEIVABLES (LINES 7 TO 9 INCL.)			10	Other	2115	
LESS: Allowance for Doubtful Accounts	1180		11	Current Amount-Long Term Debt	2117	
NET CUSTOMER RECEIVABLES (LINE 10 LESS 11)			12	TOTAL NOTES PAYABLE (LINES 7 TO 11 INCL.)		
Finance & Insurance Co. Receivables	1135		13	**ACCRUED LIABILITIES**		
Other Factory Receivables	1136		14	Interest	2120	
Factory Receivables Incentive	1137		15	Payroll	2130	
Warranty Claims Receivable-Mazda	1140		16	Insurance	2140	
Warranty Claims Receivable-Other	1141		17	Taxes-Payroll	2150	
Transportation Claims Receivable	1150		18	Taxes-Sales	2160	
Pre-Delivery Inspection	1160		19	Taxes-Other	2170	
TOTAL RECEIVABLES (LINES 12, 13 THRU 19 INCL.)			20	Income Taxes-Prior Year	2175	
INVENTORIES MEMO (CARS) (TRUCKS)			21	Income Taxes-Current Year	2177	
Demonstrators-Mazda (X)	1200		22	Bonuses-Employees	2180	
Demonstrators-Other (X)	1210		23	Bonuses-Owners	2185	
New Mazda (X)	1220		24	Pension Fund	2190	
New Other (X)	1230		25	Other	2195	
SUB TOTAL NEW & DEMO INVENTORY (LINES 22 THRU 25 INCL.)			26	Reserve for Repossession Losses	2199	
LIFO Reserve-New Vehicles	1235		27	TOTAL ACCRUED LIABILITIES (LINES 14 TO 26)		
NET NEW & DEMO INVENTORY (LINE 26 LESS 27)			28	TOTAL CURRENT LIABILITIES (LINES 6, 12, AND 27)		
Used Vehicles ( )	1240		29	**LONG TERM DEBT**		
Memo OVER 30 DAYS ( )			30	Long Term Debt	2300	
Parts & Accessories-Mazda	1250		31	Mortgages Payable-Real Estate	2310	
Parts & Accessories-Other	1260		32	Lease & Rental Vehicles	2320	
SUB TOTAL PARTS & ACCESSORIES (LINES 31 & 32)			33	Notes-Officers/Owners	2330	
LIFO Reserve-Parts & Accessories	1265		34	TOTAL LONG TERM DEBT (LINES 30 TO 33)		
NET PARTS & ACCESSORIES (LINE 33 LESS 34)			35	TOTAL LIABILITIES (LINES 28 & 34)		
Gas, Oil & Grease	1270		36	**NET WORKING CAPITAL**		
Paint & Body Shop Materials	1272		37	$		
Sublet Repairs	1275		38	(ASSETS LINE 46 MINUS LIABILITIES LINE 28)		
Work in Process-Labor	1277		39	**NET WORTH**		
Miscellaneous Inventories	1280		40	**CORPORATION ONLY**		
TOTAL INVENTORIES (LINES 28, 29, 35 TO 40)			41	PREFERRED STOCK	2800	
OTHER CURRENT ASSETS			42	COMMON STOCK	2801	1 000 000
Securities	1300		43	TREASURY STOCK	2802	
Prepaid Expense	1350	30 000	44	ADDITIONAL PAID IN CAPITAL	2805	
TOTAL OTHER CURRENT ASSETS (LINES 42 TO 44)		30 000	45	RETAINED EARNINGS	2810	
TOTAL CURRENT ASSETS (LINES 5, 20, 41, 45)		1 000 000	46	DIVIDENDS	2820	
Lease and Rental Units ( )	1420/1421		47	**PROPRIETOR OR PARTNER**		
L & R ACCUMULATED UNITS DOWN	1421		48	INVESTMENTS (JUST EACH PARTNER)	2830	
			49			
FIXED ASSETS-AUTO BUSINESS ONLY			50	DRAWINGS (JUST EACH PARTNER)	2840	

FIXED ASSETS-AUTO BUSINESS ONLY

	ACCT. NO.	COST	ACCUMULATED DEPRECIATION	LINE NO.							
LAND	1900			51							
				52							
BLDGS. & IMPROVE.	1901			53	JAN						
M&S EQUIP.	1920			54	FEB						
P&A EQUIP.	1930			55	MAR						
SHOP & TOOL	1940			56	APR						
SERVICE UNITS	1950			57	MAY						
LEASE-HOLDS	1960			58	JUN						
SIGNS	1980			59	JUL						
TOTAL (LINES 51 TO 59 INCL.)				60	AUG						
Memo-Service Units: Cars (X) Trucks				61	SEP						

OTHER ASSETS

ASSETS	ACCT. NO.	AMOUNT	LINE NO.					
			62	OCT				
Deposits	1600		63	NOV				
Life Insurance-Cash Value	1620		64	DEC				
Notes and Accounts Receivable-Officers	1630		65		**— TOTAL UNITS**			
Advances to Employees	1640		66	PROFIT OR (LOSS) BEFORE TAXES (LINES 53 TO 64 YTD)			
Other Assets & Investments	1650		67	ESTIMATED INCOME TAX (LINE 68, LESS 66)			
Other Notes & Accounts Receivable	1670		68	NET PROFIT OR (LOSS) AFTER TAXES	2850		
TOTAL OTHER ASSETS (LINES 62 TO 68 INCL.)			69	TOTAL NET WORTH (LINES 41 TO 48 INCL.)		1 000000
TOTAL ASSETS (LINES 5, 20, 41, 47, 49, 60 & 69)		1 000 000	70	TOTAL LIABILITIES & NET WORTH (LINES 35 & 69)		1 000000

FORM MAZ-030-A1 (1PN) 1/94
Reynolds+Reynolds 1-800-344-9996

OMIT CENTS

Transaction: Dealership paid $100,000 in cash for machinery, tools and equipment

    Debit: Machinery, tools and equipment $100,000

    Credit: Cash $100,000

BALANCE SHEET

Assets		Liabilities	
Cash	$ 870,000		
Prepaid Rent	$ 30,000		
Machinery, tools and equipment	$ 100,000	Net Worth Capital Stock	$1,000,000
Total Assets	$1,000,000	Total Liabilities and Net Worth	$1,000,000

DEALER FINANCIAL STATEMENT

Dealer # _______________

Region/District _______________

Sales District # _______________

COVERING PERIOD FROM _______________ THRU _______________ DEALER _______________

MAKES OTHER THAN MAZDA _______________ CITY _______________ STATE _______________

ASSETS

ASSETS	ACCT. NO.	AMOUNT	LINE NO.
CURRENT ASSETS			1
CASH			2
In Bank and on Hand	1000 / 1005	870,000	3
Contracts in Transit	1020		4
TOTAL CASH & CONTRACTS (Lines 3 to 4 incl.)		870,000	5
RECEIVABLES (MEMO PAST DUE OVER 30 DAYS)			6
Vehicle Accounts	1110		7
Service, Parts & Body Shop	1120		8
Other Customer Accounts	1130		9
TOTAL CUSTOMER RECEIVABLES (Lines 7 to 9 incl.)			10
LESS: Allowance for Doubtful Accounts	1180		11
NET CUSTOMER RECEIVABLES (Line 10 less 11)			12
Finance & Insurance Co. Receivables	1135		13
Other Factory Receivables	1136		14
Factory Receivables Incentive	1137		15
Warranty Claims Receivables-Mazda	1140		16
Warranty Claims Receivable-Other	1141		17
Transportation Claims Receivable	1150		18
Pre-Delivery Inspection	1160		19
TOTAL RECEIVABLES (Lines 12 thru 19 incl.)			20
INVENTORIES (CARS / TRUCK)			21
Demonstrators-Mazda (X)	1200		22
Demonstrators-Other (X)	1210		23
New Mazda (X)	1220		24
New Other (X)	1230		25
SUB TOTAL NEW & DEMO INVENTORY (Lines 22 thru 25 incl.)			26
LIFO Reserve-New Vehicles	1235		27
NET NEW & DEMO INVENTORY (Line 26 less 27)			28
Used Vehicles ( )	1240		29
Memo Over 90 Days ( )			30
Parts & Accessories-Mazda	1250		31
Parts & Accessories-Other	1260		32
SUB TOTAL PARTS & ACCESSORIES (Lines 31 & 32)			33
LIFO Reserve-Parts & Accessories	1265		34
NET PARTS & ACCESSORIES (Line 33 less 34)			35
Gas, Oil & Grease	1270		36
Paint & Body Shop Materials	1272		37
Sublet Repairs	1275		38
Work in Process-Labor	1277		39
Miscellaneous Inventories	1280		40
TOTAL INVENTORIES (Lines 28, 29, 35 to 40)			41
OTHER CURRENT ASSETS			42
Securities	1300		43
Prepaid Expense	1350	30,000	44
TOTAL OTHER CURRENT ASSETS (Lines 43 to 44)		30,000	45
TOTAL CURRENT ASSETS (Lines 5, 20, 41 & 45)		900,000	46
Lease and Rental Units ( )	1400 / 1401		47
L & R Accumulated Write Down	1421		48

FIXED ASSETS-AUTO BUSINESS ONLY

	ACCT. NO.	COST	ACCUMULATED DEPRECIATION	AMOUNT	LINE NO.
LAND	1500				52
BLDG. & IMPROV.	1510 / 1511				53
M & S EQUIP.	1520 / 1521	100,000		100,000	54
P & A EQUIP.	1522 / 1523				55
FURN. & FIXT.	1525 / 1526				56
SERVICE UNITS	1530 / 1531				57
LEASE HOLDS	1535 / 1536				58
SIGNS	1545 / 1546				59
TOTAL (Lines 52 to 59 incl.)				100,000	60
Memo-Service Units: Cars (X) Trucks					61

OTHER ASSETS

OTHER ASSETS	ACCT. NO.	AMOUNT	LINE NO.
Deposits	1600		63
Life Insurance-Cash Value	1620		64
Notes and Accounts Receivable-Officers	1630		65
Advances to Employees	1640		66
Other Assets & Investments	1650		67
Other Notes & Accounts Receivable	1670		68
TOTAL OTHER ASSETS (Lines 63 to 68 incl.)			69
TOTAL ASSETS (Lines 46, 47, 48, 60 & 69)		1,000,000	70

LIABILITIES

LIABILITIES	ACCT. NO.	AMOUNT	LINE NO.
CURRENT LIABILITIES			1
ACCOUNTS PAYABLE			2
Vendors	2000		3
Customers Deposits	2005		4
Other	2010		5
TOTAL ACCOUNTS PAYABLE (Lines 3 to 5 incl.)			6
NOTES PAYABLE			7
New Vehicles & Demonstrators	2100		8
Used Vehicles	2110		9
Other	2115		10
Current Amount-Long Term Debt	2117		11
TOTAL NOTES PAYABLE (Lines 8 to 11 incl.)			12
ACCRUED LIABILITIES			13
Interest	2120		14
Payroll	2130		15
Insurance	2140		16
Taxes-Payroll	2150		17
Taxes-Sales	2160		18
Taxes-Other	2170		19
Income Taxes-Prior Year	2175		20
Income Taxes-Current Year	2177		21
Bonuses-Employees	2180		22
Bonuses-Owners	2185		23
Pension Fund	2190		24
Other	2195		25
Reserve for Repossession Losses	2198		26
TOTAL ACCRUED LIABILITIES (Lines 14 to 26 incl.)			27
TOTAL CURRENT LIABILITIES (Lines 6, 12 and 27)			28
LONG TERM DEBT			29
Long Term Debt	2300		30
Mortgages Payable-Real Estate	2310		31
Lease & Rental Vehicles	2320		32
Notes-Officers/Owners	2330		33
TOTAL LONG TERM DEBT (Lines 30 to 33)			34
TOTAL LIABILITIES (Lines 28 & 34)			35

NET WORKING CAPITAL / MEMO

NET WORKING CAPITAL		AMOUNT	LINE NO.
(ASSETS Line 46 less current liabilities Line 28)	MEMO: LIFO New Veh.		36
	LIFO Parts		37
	Total LIFO Res.		38

NET WORTH

CORPORATION ONLY	ACCT. NO.	AMOUNT	LINE NO.
			39
			40
PREFERRED STOCK	2800		41
COMMON STOCK	2801	1,000,000	42
TREASURY STOCK	2802 ( )		43
ADDITIONAL PAID IN CAPITAL	2805		44
RETAINED EARNINGS	2810		45
DIVIDENDS	2820 ( )		46
PROPRIETOR OR PARTNER			47
INVESTMENTS (List Each Partner)	2830		48
			49
DRAWINGS (List Each Partner)	2840		50
			51

Monthly Profit or (Loss)

	NEW MAZDA	NEW OTHER	USED RETAIL	USED WHOLESALE	PROFIT OR (LOSS) BEFORE TAXES (INCL. 3 LES MONTHS)	LINE NO.
JAN						53
FEB						54
MAR						55
APR						56
MAY						57
JUN						58
JUL						59
AUG						60
SEP						61
OCT						62
NOV						63
DEC						64
← TOTAL UNITS						65

	ACCT. NO.	AMOUNT	LINE NO.
PROFIT OR (LOSS) BEFORE TAXES (Page 1 Line 65 YTD)			66
ESTIMATED INCOME TAX (Page 1 Line 66 YTD)			67
NET PROFIT OR (LOSS) AFTER TAXES	2850		68
TOTAL NET WORTH (Lines 41 to 68 incl.)		1,000,000	69
TOTAL LIABILITIES & NET WORTH (Line 35 + Line 69)		1,000,000	70

FORM MAZ-630-A1 (TPIO 1/94)

Reynolds+Reynolds   1-800-344-8898

OMIT CENTS

Transaction: Dealership purchased and floor-planned 100 new cars (at an average of $16,000 each) for $1,600,000

        Debit: New Car Inventory $1,600,000

        Credit: Wholesale finance liability $1,600,000

BALANCE SHEET

Assets		Liabilities	
Cash	$ 870,000	Wholesale Finance Liability- New Vehicles	$1,600,000
New Car Inventory	$1,600,000		
Prepaid Rent	$ 30,000		
Machinery, tools and equipment	$ 100,000	Net Worth Capital Stock	$1,000,000
Total Assets	$2,600,000	Total liabilities and Net Worth	$2,600,000

Note: 1) If the manufacturer includes a holdback in the invoice amount, there would be an increase in
the   Wholesale Finance Liability and a debit to a factory receivable for the like amount.
        2) In practice, the liability account for floored new units would be described as "payable."
          Technically, the note is normally not due and "payable" until the unit is sold.

DEALER FINANCIAL STATEMENT

Dealer # ______________________
Region/Distrib. ______________________
Sales District # ______________________

COVERING PERIOD FROM ______________ THRU ______________ DEALER ______________
MAKES OTHER THAN MAZDA ______________ CITY ______________ STATE ______________

	ASSETS	ACCT. NO.	AMOUNT	LINE NO.	LIABILITIES	ACCT. NO.	AMOUNT
	CURRENT ASSETS			1	**CURRENT LIABILITIES**		
	CASH			2	**ACCOUNTS PAYABLE**		
	In Bank and on Hand	1000/1003	870 000	3	Vendors	2000	
	Contracts in Transit	1020		4	Customers Deposits	2005	
	TOTAL CASH & CONTRACTS (LINES 3 TO 4 INCL.)		870 000	5	Other	2010	
	RECEIVABLES (NOT PAST DUE / OVER 30 DAYS)			6	TOTAL ACCOUNTS PAYABLE (LINES 3 TO 5 INCL.)		
	Vehicle Accounts	1110		7	**NOTES PAYABLE**		
	Service, Parts & Body Shop	1120		8	New Vehicles & Demonstrators	2100	1 600 000
	Other Customer Accounts	1130		9	Used Vehicles	2110	
	TOTAL CUSTOMER RECEIVABLES (LINES 7 TO 9 INCL.)			10	Other	2115	
	LESS: Allowance for Doubtful Accounts	1180		11	Current Amount-Long Term Debt	2117	
	NET CUSTOMER RECEIVABLES (LINE 10 LESS 11)			12	TOTAL NOTES PAYABLE (LINES 8 TO 11 INCL.)		1 600 000
	Finance & Insurance Co. Receivables	1135		13	**ACCRUED LIABILITIES**		
	Other Factory Receivables	1136		14	Interest	2120	
	Factory Receivables Incentive	1137		15	Payroll	2130	
	Warranty Claims Receivables-Mazda	1140		16	Insurance	2140	
	Warranty Claims Receivables-Other	1141		17	Taxes-Payroll	2150	
	Transportation Claims Receivable	1150		18	Taxes-Sales	2160	
	Pre-Delivery Inspection	1160		19	Taxes-Other	2170	
	TOTAL RECEIVABLES (LINES 12, 13 THRU 19 INCL.)			20	Income Taxes-Prior Year	2175	
	INVENTORIES (DAYS / TRUCKS)			21	Income Taxes-Current Year	2177	
	Demonstrators-Mazda (X)	1200		22	Bonuses-Employees	2180	
	Demonstrators-Other (X)	1210		23	Bonuses-Owners	2185	
	New Mazda (100 X)	1220	1 600 000	24	Pension Fund	2190	
	New Other (X)	1230		25	Other	2195	
	SUB TOTAL NEW & DEMO INVENTORY (LINES 22 THRU 25 INCL.)		1 600 000	26	Reserve for Repossession Losses	2199	
	LIFO Reserve-New Vehicles	1235		27	TOTAL ACCRUED LIABILITIES (LINES 14 TO 26 INCL.)		
	NET NEW & DEMO INVENTORY (LINE 26 LESS 27)			28	TOTAL CURRENT LIABILITIES (LINES 6, 12 & 27)		1 600 000
	Used Vehicles ( )	1240		29	**LONG TERM DEBT**		
	Memo (UNITS) ( )			30	Long Term Debt	2300	
	Parts & Accessories-Mazda	1250		31	Mortgages Payable-Real Estate	2310	
	Parts & Accessories-Other	1260		32	Lease & Rental Vehicles	2320	
	SUB TOTAL PARTS & ACCESSORIES (LINES 31 & 32)			33	Notes-Officers/Owners	2330	
	LIFO Reserve-Parts & Accessories	1265		34	TOTAL LONG TERM DEBT (LINES 30 TO 33)		
	NET PARTS & ACCESSORIES (LINE 33 LESS 34)			35	TOTAL LIABILITIES (LINES 28 & 34)		
	Gas, Oil & Grease	1270		36	**NET WORKING CAPITAL** — MEMO LIFO New Veh.		
	Paint & Body Shop Materials	1272		37	— LIFO Parts		
	Sublet Repairs	1275		38	— Total LIFO Res.		
	Work in Process-Labor	1277		39	**NET WORTH**		
	Miscellaneous Inventories	1280		40	**CORPORATION ONLY**		
	TOTAL INVENTORIES (LINES 28, 29, 35 TO 40)		1 600 000	41	PREFERRED STOCK	2800	
	OTHER CURRENT ASSETS			42	COMMON STOCK	2801	1 000 000
	Securities	1300		43	TREASURY STOCK	2802	
	Prepaid Expense	1350	30 000	44	ADDITIONAL PAID IN CAPITAL	2805	
	TOTAL OTHER CURRENT ASSETS (LINES 43 TO 44)		30 000	45	RETAINED EARNINGS	2810	
	TOTAL CURRENT ASSETS (LINES 5, 20, 41 & 45)		2 500 000	46	DIVIDENDS	2820	
	Lease and Rental Units ( )	1400/1401		47	**PROPRIETOR OR PARTNER**		
	L & R Accumulated Write Down	1421		48	INVESTMENTS (LIST EACH PARTNER)	2830	
				49			
	FIXED ASSETS-AUTO BUSINESS ONLY			50	DRAWINGS (LIST EACH PARTNER)	2840	

FIXED ASSETS-AUTO BUSINESS ONLY

	ACCT. NO.	COST	ACCUMULATED DEPRECIATION		LINE NO.		NEW — MAZDA	NEW — OTHER	USED — RETAIL	USED — WHOLESALE	PROFIT OR (LOSS) BEFORE TAXES (PG. 2 LINE 7)
LAND					51						
BLDGS. & IMPROV.					52						
M & S EQUIP.	1380	100 000	100 000		53	JAN					
P & A EQUIP.					54	FEB					
FURN. & FIXT.					55	MAR					
SERVICE UNITS					56	APR					
LEASEHOLDS					57	MAY					
OTHER					58	JUN					
					59	JUL					
TOTAL (LINES 52 TO 59 INCL.)			300 000		60	AUG					
* Memo.-Service Units: Cars (X) Trucks					61	SEP					

	ASSETS	ACCT. NO.	AMOUNT	LINE NO.		NEW — MAZDA	NEW — OTHER	USED — RETAIL	USED — WHOLESALE	PROFIT OR (LOSS) BEFORE TAXES
	OTHER ASSETS			62	OCT					
	Deposits	1600		63	NOV					
	Life Insurance-Cash Value	1620		64	DEC					
	Notes and Accounts Receivable-Officers	1630		65						— TOTAL UNITS
	Advances to Employees	1640		66	PROFIT OR (LOSS) BEFORE TAXES (PAGE 2, LINE 6X YTD)					
	Other Assets & Investments	1650		67	ESTIMATED INCOME TAX (PAGE 2, LINE 6X YTD)					
	Other Notes & Accounts Receivable	1670		68	NET PROFIT OR (LOSS) AFTER TAXES	2850				
	TOTAL OTHER ASSETS (LINES 63 TO 68)			69	TOTAL NET WORTH					
	TOTAL ASSETS (LINES 46, 47, 48, 49, 50, 60 & 69)		2 500 000	70	TOTAL LIABILITIES & NET WORTH					

FORM MAZ-800-A1 (TPH) 1/94
Reynolds=Reynolds 1-800-344-0000

OMIT CENTS

Transaction: Dealership purchased $200,000 worth of parts on open account.

    Debit: Parts Inventory $200,000

    Credit: Accounts Payables $200,000

BALANCE SHEET

Assets		Liabilities	
Cash	$ 870,000	Accounts Payables	$200,000
New Car Inventory	$1,600,000	Wholesale Finance	
Parts Inventory	$ 200,000	Liability - New Vehicles	$1,600,000
Prepaid Rent	$ 30,000		
Machinery, tools		Capital Stock	$1,000,000
and equipment	$ 100,000		
Total Assets	$2,800,000	Total Liabilities	
		and Net Worth	$2,800,000

DEALER FINANCIAL STATEMENT

FORM MAZ-030-A1 (1790 1/94)
Reynolds + Reynolds   1-800-364-9994

Dealer # ______________________
Region/Distrib. ______________________
Sales District # ______________________

COVERING PERIOD FROM ____________ THRU ____________ DEALER ____________
MAKES OTHER THAN MAZDA ____________ CITY ____________ STATE ____________

ASSETS

Assets	Acct. No.	Amount
CURRENT ASSETS		
CASH		
In Bank and on Hand	1000 / 1005	870 000
Contracts in Transit	1020	
TOTAL CASH & CONTRACTS		870 000
RECEIVABLES (MEMO PAST DUE OVER 30 DAYS)		
Vehicle Accounts	1110	
Service, Parts & Body Shop	1120	
Other Customer Accounts	1130	
TOTAL CUSTOMER RECEIVABLES		
LESS: Allowance for Doubtful Accounts	1180	
NET CUSTOMER RECEIVABLES		
Finance & Insurance Co. Receivables	1135	
Other Factory Receivables	1136	
Factory Receivables Incentive	1137	
Warranty Claims Receivables-Mazda	1140	
Warranty Claims Receivables-Other	1141	
Transportation Claims Receivable	1150	
Pre-Delivery Inspection	1160	
TOTAL RECEIVABLES		
INVENTORIES (CARS / TRUCKS)		
Demonstrators-Mazda (X)	1200	
Demonstrators-Other (X)	1210	
New Mazda (100 X)	1220	1 600 000
New Other (X)	1230	
SUB TOTAL NEW & DEMO INVENTORY		1 600 000
LIFO Reserve-New Vehicles	1235	
NET NEW & DEMO INVENTORY		
Used Vehicles ( )	1240	
Memo Over 30 Days ( )		
Parts & Accessories-Mazda	1250	200 000
Parts & Accessories-Other	1260	
SUB TOTAL PARTS & ACCESSORIES		
LIFO Reserve-Parts & Accessories	1265	
NET PARTS & ACCESSORIES		
Gas, Oil & Grease	1270	
Paint & Body Shop Materials	1272	
Sublet Repairs	1275	
Work In Process-Labor	1277	
Miscellaneous Inventories	1280	
TOTAL INVENTORIES		1 800 000
OTHER CURRENT ASSETS		
Securities	1300	
Prepaid Expense	1350	30 000
TOTAL OTHER CURRENT ASSETS		30 000
TOTAL CURRENT ASSETS		2 700 000
Lease and Rental Units ( )	1400 / 1401	
L & R Accumulated Write Down	1421	

FIXED ASSETS-AUTO BUSINESS ONLY

	Acct. No.	Cost	Accumulated Depreciation	
LAND	1700			
BLDGS. & IMPROV.	1750 / 1751			
M.&E. EQUIP.	1760 / 1761	100 000		100 000
P.&A. EQUIP.	1770 / 1771			
FURN. & FIXT.	1780 / 1781			
SERVICE UNITS	1790 / 1791			
LEASE-HOLDS	1795 / 1796			
SIGNS	1798 / 1799			
TOTAL				

* Memo.-Service Units: Cars (X) Trucks

OTHER ASSETS

Other Assets	Acct. No.	Amount
Deposits	1600	
Life Insurance-Cash Value	1620	
Notes and Accounts Receivable-Officers	1630	
Advances to Employees	1640	
Other Assets & Investments	1650	
Other Notes & Accounts Receivable	1670	
TOTAL OTHER ASSETS		
TOTAL ASSETS		2 800 000

LIABILITIES

Line No.	Liabilities	Acct. No.	Amount
1	**CURRENT LIABILITIES**		
2	**ACCOUNTS PAYABLE**		
3	Vendors	2000	200 000
4	Customers Deposits	2005	
5	Other	2010	
6	TOTAL ACCOUNTS PAYABLE		200 000
7	**NOTES PAYABLE**		
8	New Vehicles & Demonstrators	2100	1 500 000
9	Used Vehicles	2110	
10	Other	2115	
11	Current Amount-Long Term Debt	2117	
12	TOTAL NOTES PAYABLE		1 500 000
13	**ACCRUED LIABILITIES**		
14	Interest	2120	
15	Payroll	2130	
16	Insurance	2140	
17	Taxes-Payroll	2150	
18	Taxes-Sales	2160	
19	Taxes-Other	2170	
20	Income Taxes-Prior Year	2175	
21	Income Taxes-Current Year	2177	
22	Bonuses-Employees	2180	
23	Bonuses-Owners	2185	
24	Pension Fund	2190	
25	Other	2195	
26	Reserve for Repossession Losses	2199	
27	TOTAL ACCRUED LIABILITIES		
28	TOTAL CURRENT LIABILITIES		1 800 000
29	**LONG TERM DEBT**		
30	Long Term Debt	2300	
31	Mortgages Payable-Real Estate	2310	
32	Lease & Rental Vehicles	2320	
33	Notes-Officers/Owners	2330	
34	TOTAL LONG TERM DEBT		
35	TOTAL LIABILITIES		
36	NET WORKING CAPITAL		
37	$		
38	(ASSETS LINE 46 MINUS LIABILITIES LINE 28)		
39	**NET WORTH**		
40	**CORPORATION ONLY**		
41	PREFERRED STOCK	2800	
42	COMMON STOCK	2801	1 000 000
43	TREASURY STOCK	2802	
44	ADDITIONAL PAID IN CAPITAL	2805	
45	RETAINED EARNINGS	2810	
46	DIVIDENDS	2820	
47	**PROPRIETOR OR PARTNER**		
48	INVESTMENTS (LIST EACH PARTNER)	2830	
49			
50	DRAWINGS (LIST EACH PARTNER)	2840	
51			

MEMO: LIFO New Veh. ___ / LIFO Parts ___ / Total LIFO Res. ___

Line No.	Month	NEW Mazda	NEW Other	USED Retail	USED Wholesale	PROFIT OR (LOSS) BEFORE TAXES (PG. 2 LINE 24 MONTH)
52						
53	JAN					
54	FEB					
55	MAR					
56	APR					
57	MAY					
58	JUN					
59	JUL					
60	AUG					
61	SEP					
62	OCT					
63	NOV					
64	DEC					
65						— TOTAL UNITS

Line No.	Liabilities	Acct. No.	Amount
66	PROFIT OR (LOSS) BEFORE TAXES (PAGE 2 LINE 24 YTD)		
67	ESTIMATED INCOME TAX (PAGE 2 LINE 25 YTD)		
68	NET PROFIT OR (LOSS) AFTER TAXES	2850	
69	TOTAL NET WORTH		000 000
70	TOTAL LIABILITIES & NET WORTH		2 800 000

OMIT CENTS

The balance sheet now presents a picture of the dealership's assets and capital structure before any sales of merchandise have been made. Total assets are now $2,800,000. Total liabilities and Net Worth are $2,800,000. With the sale of a car by the dealership, it becomes necessary to supplement the balance sheet analysis.

Transaction: Dealership sold a new unit for $17,200 (costing $16,000) receiving $2,500 in cash and a used car for $8,000.

Initially:

    Cash increases $2,500
    Contracts in Transit increases $6,700
    Used Car Inventory increases $8,000
    New Car Inventory decreases $16,000
    Earning increase by ($17,200 - $16,000) = $1,200

After the car invoice is paid:

    Cash decreases $16,000
    New Vehicle Payables decreases $16,000

BALANCE SHEET

Assets		Liabilities	
Cash	$ 856,500	Accounts payables	$ 200,000
Contracts in Transit	$ 6,700	Wholesale Finance	
New Car Inventory	$1,584,000	Liability-New Units	$1,584,000
Used Car Inventory	$ 8,000		
Parts Inventory	$ 200,000	Capital Stock	$1,000,000
Prepaid Rent	$ 30,000	Earnings	$ 1,200
Machinery, tools		Net Worth	$1,001,200
and equipment	$ 100,000		
Total Assets	$2,785,200	Total Liabilities	
		and Net Worth	$2,785,200

DEALER FINANCIAL STATEMENT

Dealer # _______________
Region/Distrib. _______________
Sales District # _______________

COVERING PERIOD FROM _____________ THRU _____________ DEALER _______________
MAKES OTHER THAN MAZDA _____________ CITY _____________ STATE _______________

ASSETS	ACCT. NO.	AMOUNT	LINE NO.	LIABILITIES	ACCT. NO.	AMOUNT
CURRENT ASSETS			1	**CURRENT LIABILITIES**		
CASH			2	**ACCOUNTS PAYABLE**		
In Bank and on Hand	1000-1003	856 500	3	Vendors	2000	200 000
Contracts in Transit	1020	6 700	4	Customers Deposits	2005	
TOTAL CASH & CONTRACTS		863 200	5	Other	2010	
RECEIVABLES (MEMO PAST DUE OVER 30 DAYS)			6	TOTAL ACCOUNTS PAYABLE		200 000
Vehicle Accounts	1110		7	**NOTES PAYABLE**		
Service, Parts & Body Shop	1120		8	New Vehicles & Demonstrators	2100	1 584 000
Other Customer Accounts	1130		9	Used Vehicles	2110	
TOTAL CUSTOMER RECEIVABLES			10	Other	2115	
LESS: Allowance for Doubtful Accounts	1180		11	Current Amount-Long Term Debt	2117	
NET CUSTOMER RECEIVABLES			12	TOTAL NOTES PAYABLE		1 584 000
Finance & Insurance Co. Receivables	1135		13	**ACCRUED LIABILITIES**		
Other Factory Receivables	1136		14	Interest	2120	
Factory Receivables Incentive	1137		15	Payroll	2130	
Warranty Claims Receivable-Mazda	1140		16	Insurance	2140	
Warranty Claims Receivable-Other	1141		17	Taxes-Payroll	2150	
Transportation Claims Receivable	1150		18	Taxes-Sales	2160	
Pre-Delivery Inspection	1160		19	Taxes-Other	2170	
TOTAL RECEIVABLES			20	Income Taxes-Prior Year	2175	
INVENTORIES (CAR / TRUCK)			21	Income Taxes-Current Year	2177	
Demonstrators-Mazda ( )( )	1200		22	Bonuses-Employees	2180	
Demonstrators-Other ( )( )	1210		23	Bonuses-Owners	2185	
New Mazda (99)( )	1220	1 584000	24	Pension Fund	2190	
New Other ( )( )	1230		25	Other	2195	
SUB TOTAL NEW & DEMO INVENTORY		1 584000	26	Reserve for Repossession Losses	2199	
LIFO Reserve-New Vehicles	1235		27	TOTAL ACCRUED LIABILITIES		
NET NEW & DEMO INVENTORY			28	TOTAL CURRENT LIABILITIES		1 784 000
Used Vehicles (1)	1240	8000	29	**LONG TERM DEBT**		
Memo OVER 60 DAYS ( )			30	Long Term Debt	2300	
Parts & Accessories-Mazda	1250	200000	31	Mortgages Payable-Real Estate	2310	
Parts & Accessories-Other	1260		32	Lease & Rental Vehicles	2320	
SUB TOTAL PARTS & ACCESSORIES			33	Notes-Officers/Owners	2330	
LIFO Reserve-Parts & Accessories	1265		34	TOTAL LONG TERM DEBT		
NET PARTS & ACCESSORIES			35	TOTAL LIABILITIES		
Gas, Oil & Grease	1270		36	**NET WORKING CAPITAL**	MEMO LIFO New Veh.	
Paint & Body Shop Materials	1272		37	$	MEMO LIFO Parts	
Sublet Repairs	1275		38	CURRENT-TIME CURRENT LIABILITIES LINE 28	MEMO Total LIFO Res.	
Work in Process-Labor	1277		39	**NET WORTH**		
Miscellaneous Inventories	1280		40	**CORPORATION ONLY**		
TOTAL INVENTORIES		1 792000	41	PREFERRED STOCK	2800	
OTHER CURRENT ASSETS			42	COMMON STOCK	2801	1 000 000
Securities	1300		43	TREASURY STOCK	2802	( )
Prepaid Expense	1350	30000	44	ADDITIONAL PAID IN CAPITAL	2805	
TOTAL OTHER CURRENT ASSETS		30000	45	RETAINED EARNINGS	2810	
TOTAL CURRENT ASSETS		2 685200	46	DIVIDENDS	2820	( )
Lease and Rental Units ( )	1400 / 1401		47	**PROPRIETOR OR PARTNER**		
L & R ACCUMULATED WRITE DOWN	1421		48	INVESTMENTS (LIST EACH PARTNER)	2830	
			49			

FIXED ASSETS-AUTO BUSINESS ONLY

	ACCT. NO.	COST	ACCUMULATED DEPRECIATION		LINE NO.		NEW		USED		PROFIT OR (LOSS) BEFORE TAXES (INCL. 2 LAST MONTH)
							MAZDA	OTHER	RETAIL	WHOLESALE	
LAND	1500				50	DRAWINGS (LIST EACH PARTNER) 2840					
					51						
					52						
BLDGS. & IMPROVE. 1620					53	JAN					
M & S EQUIP. 1620		100 000		100000	54	FEB					
P & A EQUIP. 1630					55	MAR					
FURN. & FIXT. 1630					56	APR					
SERVICE UNITS 1630					57	MAY					
LEASE-HOLDS 1660 / 1661					58	JUN					
SIGNS 1440					59	JUL					
TOTAL (LINES 52 TO 59 INCL.)				100000	60	AUG					
Memo.-Service Units: Cars ( )( ) Trucks					61	SEP					

OTHER ASSETS	ACCT. NO.	AMOUNT	LINE NO.					
			62	OCT				
Deposits	1600		63	NOV				
Life Insurance-Cash Value	1620		64	DEC				
Notes and Accounts Receivable-Officers	1630		65	— TOTAL UNITS				
Advances to Employees	1640		66	PROFIT OR (LOSS) BEFORE TAXES (PAGE 2, LINE 62 YTD)				12 00
Other Assets & Investments	1650		67	ESTIMATED INCOME TAX (PAGE 2, LINE 63 YTD)				
Other Notes & Accounts Receivable	1670		68	NET PROFIT OR (LOSS) AFTER TAXES	2850			
TOTAL OTHER ASSETS (LINES 63 TO 68 INCL.)			69	TOTAL NET WORTH (LINES 41 TO 68 INCL.)		1 001 200		
TOTAL ASSETS (LINES 46, 47, 48, 69 & 60)		2 785200	70	TOTAL LIABILITIES & NET WORTH (LINES 35 & 69)		2 785 200		

OMIT CENTS

These examples have covered the basic principles of dealership accounting and how a series of dealership transactions are reflected on the debit and credit side of a balance sheet, as well as how they relate to the dealership's assets and liabilities.

BEYOND THE DEALER'S BALANCE SHEET

The first section of the financial statement, the **Balance Sheet**, reveals at a glance the financial condition of the dealership. To the prepared eye, it is often sufficient for the detection of out-of-line situations requiring corrective action. To analyze the exact cause of the condition and isolate the area requiring corrective action, the second and third sections of the financial statement are necessary.

The second section of the financial statement is known as the **Income and Expense** section. (Referred to in the accountant's language as the **Profit and Loss Statement**). Included in it is a detailed accounting of the dealership's expenses, gross profit or loss, and net profit or loss. This accounting is in terms of the dealership as a whole. However, part of this section also includes the same accounting, only it's broken out by individual department. Those include New Car, Used Car, Lease and Rental, Service, Body Shop, Parts, and General and Administrative.

While the balance of this chapter will review revenue-generating departments, it's important to understand General and Administrative (G&A). G&A refers to those expenses (office personnel, certain supplies such as checks and computer paper, and other services) that are used by all departments. These expenses are not easily identifiable in terms of how much of the cost of each item can be attributed to the department that used them. Therefore, G&A often has its own section within the Income and Expense statement. The total expense is then divided among the different departments and is found as a line item after net profit before taxes and bonus. Dealerships differ on how they divide the G&A expense. Some methods include:

- Departmental percent of the total operating revenue of the dealership, e.g. if the new car department generates 60% of the total sales, 60% of G&A is charged against the new car department
- Percent of departmental assets
- Percent of net income to overall dealership net

Whatever the method of expense division, it is still wise to account for G&A separately. In the past, many dealerships would divide each and every expense account, attributable to G&A, into each of the profit-generating departments. This only added extra accounting entry work. It also limited the Dealer's ability to see what the true costs were of administering dealership operations. In addition, it limits the accountability of the business manager over his or her own departmental expenses.

The Income and Expense section of every dealership's financial statement, regardless of franchise, is divided into two columns where totals are entered. One is the **Current Month** and the other is the **Year-to-Date** column.

The heading of each column defines its function. Thus, if the Income and Expense section covered the period from the first of the year to the end of March, the Current Month column would contain totals for the periods from March 1 to March 31 inclusive. The Year-to-Date column would contain totals for the period from January 1 to March 31 inclusive.

The third section of the Financial Statement, known as the Departmental Gross Profit Analysis Section, is in reality supplemental to the Profit and Loss statement. Thus the Net Sales and Gross Profit totals which appear in the second section (Income and Expenses) are obtained from the third section, (Departmental Gross Profit Analysis) where each of the totals is detailed. Here, each of the major departments of the dealership operation is detailed, including two major factors of the income and expense (profit or loss) picture: Sales and Gross Profit. It will be recalled that sales is defined as the selling price of merchandise or services sold. Gross profit is the difference between sales and cost-of-sales.

Of course, there is a vast difference between gross profit and operating profit, a difference made up of all the expenditures incurred by the dealership in the normal course of doing business. All expenditures must be deducted from the gross profit before operating profit or loss can be determined.

Variable Selling Expense

Variable Selling Expense represents those expenses incurred by the dealership that vary with the number of vehicles sold. Included are such expenses as:

- Sales commissions, including incentives paid to new and used car salespeople
- The cost of labor and materials spent on cars previously delivered, for which neither the factory not the customer is charged (policy work-vehicles)
- Other variable selling expenses, such as special commissions or incentives paid to salespeople, the cost of periodic inspections of new vehicles, and various small customer accommodations

In contrast to these expenses which vary with the volume of sales, there are expenses that remain relatively constant regardless of sales volume. In the financial statement, expenses which do not vary with the volume of sales are generally categorized as personnel, semi-fixed and fixed expenses. Together these expenses are called fixed overhead.

Personnel and Semi-fixed Expenses

The **Personnel** and **Semi-Fixed Expense** category includes:

- Salaries, exclusive of any bonuses paid to the Dealer and supervisory staff
- Wages paid to every dealership employee not on a commission basis
- The cost of contributing to any employee benefit plan such as hospitalization, group life, retirement plans
- Absentee wages of technicians whose services are not available due to absence caused by illness, on vacation or attending service schools
- The cost of all local advertising (sometimes included in variable expenses)
- The cost of maintaining and operating demonstrators
- Maintenance and upkeep of company cars other than demonstrators, parts trucks, service cars, and driver training cars
- Data processing
- Contributions
- Membership dues
- Necessary business travel and entertainment

- Legal and auditing fees
- Postage
- Telephone and telegraph expenses
- The cost of keeping used cars in a salable condition after they have been reconditioned, such as washing, polishing, gas and other special needs

The factory manuals followed by Dealers in the interest of uniform accounting procedures generally specify all the above items as semi-fixed expenses. Any variation which may exist between one's manual list and that of another is relatively minor.

FIXED EXPENSES

Fixed Expenses covers those costs which are constant regardless of business conditions. The category generally includes:

- Rent, including any taxes or insurance paid by the dealership as one of the conditions of the lease agreement. If the Dealer is buying rather than renting the property (rent equivalent expense) - that is, the expense of maintenance, depreciation, insurance, taxes, plus any improvements must be included in this category
- Utilities
- All insurance premiums other than those for life and group health
- All taxes other than real estate or income taxes
- The cost of maintenance and repair of all dealership equipment other than service cars and trucks
- Depreciation other than that of building and improvements

DEPARTMENTAL GROSS PROFIT ANALYSIS SECTION

This section of the Financial Statement provides the most detailed analysis of the dealership's profit or loss. As noted earlier, each of the major departments within the dealership - New Car, Used Car, Lease and Rental, Parts and Accessories, Service and Body Shop - are listed separately. Sales for each department, and the resulting gross, are entered on a current month and year-to-date basis, the same as in the preceding section.

Gross profit from new and used car sales is referred to as Variable Gross Profit, since it fluctuates as the new and used car markets fluctuate. Gross profit from parts and accessories and from service and body shop departments are referred to as Fixed Gross Profit, since income from these departments is relatively constant from month to month.

New Car and Truck Department

Within each franchise, there are different models of cars and trucks. For each model there is a particular line provided under the New Vehicle heading in the Departmental Gross Profit Analysis section of the financial statement. Within the New Vehicle Section are two sub-divided sections: **New Car and New Truck**. Each line provides space for the entry of sales and resulting gross profit. Also recorded is **the Average Gross Profit Per New Unit Sold**, obtained by dividing total gross for each line by the number of cars sold in that line. This allows the Dealer to see at a glance which models provides higher grosses, and which one lower.

A separate category confined only to fleet sales may be included in the new car section of the Gross Profit Analysis, since gross on fleet sales is usually minimal. The lack of distinction between fleet gross and retail gross would not provide a true picture of the average retail gross profit picture. Because of the growth in leasing, some dealerships segregate the sales of brokered leases, vehicles leased through manufacturers finance divisions or banks, but accounted for as a sale because they are not leased directly by the dealership. Some Dealers record these sales within the new vehicle sections, while others record this directly in the lease and rental section. However, the Lease and Rental section was originally designed to account for those units actually leased by the dealership, often referred to as in-house leases.

Also included in the vehicle sections are areas listing gross profit from finance and insurance. This is done on our sample statement.

Used Car Department

Obviously, it is neither practical nor necessary to account for used car sales on the basis of make or model, as is done with new cars. Therefore, under the Used Car heading the only distinctions made are between wholesale and retail sales and used car - used truck.

In either case, **Sales** represents the amount for which the car is sold; **Cost** represents the amount paid by the Dealer in buying the car, either as an outright wholesale purchase or, more often, as a trade-in. The financial statement used by most franchises separates the cost of reconditioning used cars.

A generally accepted practice is adjusting the value of used cars in inventory on a monthly basis to account for changes in wholesale market value and to adjust for depreciation of units that have not sold at previously determined prices.

Parts and Accessories Department

In the type of financial statement ordinarily used by Dealers, parts and accessories sales and gross profit are listed on an autonomous basis. Categories from which a gross profit is obtained include parts-counter retail; parts-repair orders; parts-factory claims; parts-wholesale; and parts-internal. Tires, gas, oil and grease, and miscellaneous items form an additional classification.

Service Department

Under the service department heading, Ford and Lincoln/Mercury Dealers originally computed the gross on Customer Repairs, Body and Paint, Warranty and Policy Claims, and Sublet Repairs. General Motors Dealers had these same categories plus labor-internal, and the cost of productive labor (technicians) which the Dealer paid for but did not see. Ford has added Labor-Internal.

Both financial statements end up combining the parts and accessories gross with that of the service and body shop departments to obtain the dealership's total fixed gross profit. Thus financial statements serve to illustrate a point noted earlier - that although the physical layout of one may differ somewhat from the other, the end result in terms of information obtained is similar.

Lease and Rental

This section is usually devoted to those dealerships actively involved in the leasing or renting of their own vehicles. This means the dealership actually holds title to the vehicle, and bills a customer directly for the cost of renting or leasing.

Because vehicle acquisition costs can be high, Dealers must almost always borrow the capital to purchase vehicles that will be placed in lease or rental service. This section accounts for the income from customer billings, as well as expenses such as depreciation, interest on borrowed capital, insurance, and other direct (cost-of-sale-type) expenses.

PROFIT CENTERING

Profit centering in the automobile dealership is an operating concept whereby all revenue-producing departments of the organization are considered a separate business. Each department has its own profit objective and is operated by a department manager responsible for developing necessary procedures (consistent with overall dealership policy) to produce a maximum profit contribution to the organization. Each department manager's performance is measured against a profit and sales objective established by dealership management.

The workbook in back of the text outlines various analyses of each department to assist in determining that profit center's evaluation of performance. The analyses evaluate the success of the profit center's manager in operating the department. These analyses are compared to past periods, dealership group composites (averages), stated objectives, and industry guides to further pinpoint the profit center's success as a separate entity.

Profit centering represents a constant test of how well each operating department is able to stand on its own feet as a business in and of itself. Each profit center is credited with the revenue, as well as charged with the expenses, for which it is responsible. As an example, internal work is performed at a mark-up instead of being transferred between departments at cost. The amount in excess of cost is then credited to the service department as gross profit.

Such adjustments are made only on the profit centering record. They do not affect the dealership's other accounting records, nor do they change the overall profit of the organization. They do provide a more accurate picture of the contribution each department makes to the total profit of the organization.

Additions and Deductions

In the dealership, sales and leasing of new cars, trucks, and used cars, and sales of labor, parts and accessories, and related supplies are the normal merchandising activity. After costs and expenses are deducted from these sales, the operating profit or loss is determined. This profit or loss is the measure of the success of management of these profit centers in terms of the costs and expense that resulted in the sales volume. In turn, this profit from the merchandising in these departments should represent a satisfactory return on the owner's invested capital.

In addition to the normal operating profit or loss, there may be other sources of profit or loss. In dealership accounting, these sources are classified as additions to income and deductions from income. Many policy manuals include losses due to bad debts along with miscellaneous items in this section.

Although floor plan interest used to be placed in this section, it is now more common to place floor plan expense in the semi-fixed section of the statement.

This part of the operating statement shows the items that add to the total additions to income for the month and year-to-date. Similarly, it provides for the total deductions from income. These totals are combined. The net additions and deductions are combined with the departmental operating profit or loss to indicate the profit or loss before bonuses and income taxes for the dealership.

REPRESENTATIVE JOURNAL ENTRIES AND THE ACCOUNTING CYCLE

The data that are shown on the Financial Statement come from the general ledger, subsidiary ledgers and schedules taken from the journals. Now that the ultimate destination of such entries in the financial statement has been noted, a review of how entries are accounted for and recorded in appropriate journals is in order. Following are several examples of transactions involving major departments of the dealership, together with a specific indication of the journals in which the transaction would be recorded:

New Car Department

Transaction: John Smith placed an order for a new car with a cash deposit of $1,000.

Dr.	Cash	$1,000	
Cr.	Customer Deposits		$1,000

(Debit reflects the increase in cash. Credit reflects the dealership's liability to the customer for the deposit.)

The source document is the cash receipt. The transaction is recorded in the cash receipts journal and a subsidiary record is made in the customer deposits ledger.

Transaction: The dealership purchased and received a new car from the factory.

Dr.	Inventory - New Vehicles	$16,000	
Cr.	Wholesale Finance Liability - New Vehicles		$16,000

(Debit reflects the increase in new vehicle inventory. Credit reflects the increase in the Dealership's liability - floor plan - on the vehicle.)

The source document is the factory invoice. The transaction is recorded in the new vehicle purchase journal.

Transaction: The dealership sold the new car to John Smith on a conditional sales contract.

(Sale)

Dr.	Contracts in Transit	$10,205	
	Customer Deposits	$ 1,000	
	Due from Financing Institution	$ 200	
	Inventory - Used Vehicles	$ 6,000	
Cr.	Sales - New Vehicles		$17,200
	Accrued Sales Tax		$ 860
	Accrued License and Title Tax		$ 95
	Finance and Insurance Income		$ 200

(Debits reflect increase of finance contracts in transit to the finance company, the decrease in the dealership's liability for the customer deposit, the increase in used car inventory, and the increase in finance reserve. Credits reflect the sale of the new car, including finance and insurance income, and the liability for vehicle taxes collected from the customer.)

| Dr. | Cost of Sales - New vehicles | $16,000 | |
| Cr. | Inventory - New Vehicles | | $16,000 |

(Debit reflects the cost of the new car. Credit reflects the decrease in new car inventory.)

(Sales tax, license and title fees)

Dr.	Accrued Sales Taxes	$860	
	Accrued License and Title Tax	$ 95	
Cr.	Cash		$955

(Debit reflects the decrease in liability for the sales tax and title fees collected from the customer. Credit reflects the decrease in cash.)

The source documents are the Retail Customer Invoice and the dealership's check for $280 to the Secretary of State's office. The transaction is recorded in the New Vehicle Sales journal - Retail and in the Cash Disbursement and Purchase journal. Subsidiary records are made in the vehicle inventory record, and in the customer deposits subsidiary ledger.

Transaction: The dealership paid off the Wholesale Finance Liability on the new car.

| Dr. | Wholesale Finance Liability - New Vehicles $16,000 | |
| Cr. | Cash | $16,000 |

(Debit reflects the decrease in floor plan liability on the new car sold. Credit reflects the decrease in cash.)

The source document is the dealership's check for $16,000 to the finance company. The transaction is recorded in the cash disbursements and purchase journal, with a subsidiary record in the vehicle inventory record.

The foregoing examples complete the cycle of financial transactions involving the New Vehicle Departments, beginning with the customer ordering the new vehicle and ending with the dealership paying off the floor plan on the vehicle. However, the customer traded in the old car on the new one, and until the trade-in is disposed of, the cycle of transactions generated by the new car order really cannot be regarded as entirely completed.

Used Car Department

The trade-in provides the examples of transactions involving the dealership's used car operation which follow:

Transaction: The trade-in is reconditioned be the dealership.

(Internal Sale)

| Dr. | Inventory - Used Vehicles | $205 | |
| Cr. | Inventory - Labor - Internal | | $205 |

(Debit reflects the increase in inventory value of the used vehicle. Credit reflects the sale of reconditioning labor performed.)

(Cost of Sale)
Dr.   Cost of Sales - Labor - Internal $165
Cr.   Inventory - Work in Process - Labor $165
(Debit reflects the cost of internal labor. Credit reflects the relief of inventory to which all service labor is charged.)

The source document is the internal repair order. The transaction is recorded in the Internal Sales journal and a subsidiary record is made in the Vehicle Inventory record.

Transaction: The reconditioned trade-in is sold for cash.

(Sale)
Dr.   Cash Sales $8,545
Cr.   Sales - Used Vehicles - Retail $8,000
        Accrued Sales Tax* $ 480
        Accrued License and Title Tax* $ 65
(Debit reflects the increase in asset account used to clear all cash sales. Credits reflect the sale of the used car, the liability for payment of sales tax, and the liability for payment of license and title fees.)

(Cost of Sale)
Dr.   Cost of Sale
        Used Passenger - Retail $6,500
        Reconditioning - Used Vehicles $ 205
Cr.   Inventory - Used Vehicles $6,705
(Debit reflects the cost of the used car sold. Credit reflects the dollar decrease in the used vehicle inventory.)

* These amounts may or may not be immediately "payable" depending on the law, although the accounts in practice are titled "Payable."

(Receipts of Cash)
Dr.   Cash on Hand $8,545
Cr.   Cash Sales $8,545
(Debit reflects the increase in cash. Credit reflects the decrease in the cash sales clearing account.)

(Payment of Tax and License Fees)
Dr.   Accrued Sales Tax $480
        Accrued License and Title Tax   65
Cr.   Cash on Deposit $545
(Debit reflects the payment of tax and license fees and a decrease in liability for them. Credit reflects the decrease in cash.)

Source documents are the customer invoice, cash receipt for $6,150 to the buyer, and the dealership's check for $545 to the Secretary of State office. The transaction is recorded in the Used Vehicle Sales journal, Cash Receipts journal, Cash Disbursement and Purchase journals. Subsidiary records are made in the Vehicle Inventory record.

Service Department

The next examples consist of transaction records which have to do with the service department.

Transaction: The dealership sold service labor on a repair order, accepting an approved customer account receivable in payment. The account receivable was subsequently paid.

    (Sale)
Dr.	Customer Accounts Receivables	$150	
Cr.	Sales - Customer Labor		$150

(Debit reflects the increase in customer accounts receivable. Credit reflects the amount of labor sold on the customer's repair order.)

    (Cost of Sales)
Dr.	Cost of Sales - Customer Labor	$60	
Cr.	Inventory - Work in Process - Labor		$60

(Debit reflects the cost of the customer labor performed. Credit reflects the compensation paid for productive labor sold on the completed repair order and relief of inventory as previously noted.)

Source documents are the repair order and the cash receipt for $150 to the customer. The transaction is recorded in the Service and Parts Sales journal and in the Cash Receipts journal. A subsidiary record is made in the Customer Accounts Receivables subsidiary ledger.

Transaction: Warranty work performed on a new vehicle previously sold by the dealership. The warranty claim was approved and paid by the factory.

    (Sale)
Dr.	Factory Claims	$265	
Cr.	Sales - Warranty Claims - Labor		$90
	Sales - Warranty Claims - Parts		$175

(Debit reflects the increase in factory receivables. Credits reflect the detailed sales price of warranty labor and parts.)

    (Cost of Sales)
Dr.	Cost of Sales - Warranty Claims - Labor $45		
	Cost of Sales - Warranty Claims - Parts	$120	
Cr.	Inventory - Work in Process - Labor		$45
	Inventory - Parts		$120

(Debit reflect the detailed cost of warranty labor and parts. Credits reflect the relief of labor inventory previously noted and decrease in parts inventory)

(Check Received from Factory)
Dr.   Cash $265
Cr.   Factory Claims $265
(Debit reflects the increase in cash. Debit reflects the decrease in factory claims receivables)

Source documents are the repair order and the cash receipt. The transaction is recorded in the Service Sales journal, the Claims register and in the Cash Receipts journal.

Parts Department

The next example consists of transactions involving the dealership's parts department:

Transaction: The dealership purchased parts on open account from the wholesaler and paid the account by the end of the month.

(Purchase)
Dr.   Inventory - Parts $1,100
Cr.   Accounts Payables $1,100
(Debit reflects the increase in parts inventory. Credit reflects the increase in accounts payables.)

(Payment of Account)
Dr.   Accounts Payables $1,100
Cr.   Cash $1,078
       Cash Discount Earned $ 22
(Debit reflects the decrease in accounts payables. Credits reflect the decrease in cash and the discount earned for payment of bills within a specified time.)

Source documents are the accounts payable - voucher envelope, and the dealership's check for $1,078. The transaction is recorded in the cash disbursements and purchase journals.

Transaction: Parts sold by the dealership on open account to an independent garage.

(Sale)
Dr.   Customer Receivables $135
Cr.   Sales - Parts - Wholesale $135
(Debit reflects the increase in customer accounts receivables. Credit reflects the sale of the parts wholesale.)

(Cost of Sales)
Dr.   Cost of Sales - Parts - Wholesale $108
Cr.   Inventory - Parts $108
(Debit reflects the cost of the part sold. Credit reflects the decrease in inventory-parts)

Source documents are the Parts Invoice and the cash receipt. The transactions recorded in the Service and Parts Sales journal and in the Cash Receipts journal, with a subsidiary record in the Customer Accounts Receivables ledger.

Usually, at the end of the month, the operating accounts are closed. The sales, cost of sales and expense accounts are for a definite period of time, while balance sheet accounts are as of the last day of the period. The closing process consists of transferring the opening account balances to a profit and loss summary account. The balance in the summary account represents the profit or loss for the period. A credit balance shows a net profit and a debit balance shows a net loss. The resulting balance is transferred to the investment account. (Retained Earnings is a profit)

The sales account balance is transferred to the profit and loss summary by debiting sales and crediting the profit and loss summary. The cost and expense balances are transferred to the profit and loss summary by debiting the profit and loss summary and crediting the cost and expense accounts. The credit balance in the profit and loss summary represents the net profit and is transferred to the investment account by debiting the profit and loss summary and crediting the investment account, thus increasing the balance. The operating accounts, as a result of the closing process, have now balanced and are thus closed. A new group of operating accounts will be used to record sales, cost of sales and expense transactions for the following period.

In review, this chapter has covered these parts of the dealership's financial statement - namely, the income and expense section also known as the profit and loss statement, and the departmental gross profit analysis section. Covered in these sections were such items as Variable Selling Expense; Semi-Fixed Expense; and Fixed Expense; Departmental Gross Profit Analysis of the major departments in the dealership, a review of the practice known as profit centering, and examples of transactions involving each of the major departments in the dealership. Also referenced was their effect on the debit and credit picture of the financial statement and the journals and ledgers in which they were recorded prior to inclusion in the financial statement.

To this point, the emphasis has not been in interpretation. However, analysis and interpretation of the financial statement is the most vital service that the business manager performs in his function as the dealership's accountant. It is this facet of the business manager's duties which will be covered subsequently.

CHAPTER 3

CHAPTER III

EXPENSE CONTROL

The Logic of Expense Control

Many businesses, and dealerships in particular, tend to think about increasing profits through increased sales volumes and higher gross profits.   However, the control of expenses in any business can often mean the difference between a satisfactory or unsatisfactory return, or even a loss.

If two dealerships with identical sales volumes and gross profit margins could be found, with the exception that one implemented sound expense controls and the other didn't, there would be a considerable difference in net profit results between the two. Expense control is not a sometime activity. Expenses must be under control at all times! The importance of expense control can best be shown by the below example, demonstrating the relation to net profit before taxes as a percent of total sales dollars.

The average dealership in the United States (Domestic and Import) from 1988 through 1994 averaged 1.4% (net profit before taxes as a percent of total sales) during that period. The range was a 1.8% high in 1994 to a low of 1.0% in 1989, 1990 and 1991. It has increased currently to a number slightly over 2%. The importance of controlling expenses can best be shown by the following table assuming a 2% net profit before taxes to total sales relationship.

Sales Needed to Compensate
For an Increase in Typical Expenses
at a 2% Return on Net Sales

Expense Increase	Sales Needed to Compensate
- one postage stamp	$ 16.00*
- a one dollar theft	$ 50.00
- a discount of $12 on a part	$ 600.00
- a $50 uncollected bill	$ 2,500.00
- a $350 parts shrinkage	$ 17,500.00
- a $12,000 excessive payroll	$600,000.00

* .32 divided by .02 = $16.00 etc.

Using the same 2% net profit before taxes as a percent of the sales, it can readily be seen that if you would reduce expenses by $12,000 it would have the same effect on net profit as an increase of $600,000 in sales. Increasing sales by that kind of volume would certainly be a difficult, if not an impossible, task. This is the essence of Expense Control!

Expense Control Management

The management of expenses requires five basic functions:

- Established policies
- Analysis
- Planning
- Assignment
- Evaluation

<u>Policies</u>

Written policies should be established regarding expense control. Placing such policies in writing minimizes disputes when problems arise. Written policies also demonstrate the importance the Dealer places on expense control. Policies should include expense account budget limitations with controls, requiring Dealer approval for those amounts exceeding budget. It's important to be sure that the policies do not hinder a manager's ability to make decisions that are a normal part of their day-to-day activities. Managers should be empowered to perform their jobs. Generally, policies should allow department managers to make expenditures necessary to operate their departments, providing they remain within budget forecasts. Defined limits should be placed on expenses, such as purchases of capital equipment, tools, special training, or other items that do not have an immediate impact on everyday business. Examples of day-to-day expenses include purchasing office supplies, repair order purchases, used vehicles (providing total inventory budgets are adhered to), gas, parts, paint supplies, etc.

<u>Analysis</u>

All expense accounts should be analyzed, particularly those with larger costs or balances. They should be compared against Dealer group composites (averages) and past historical performance. This will aid in determining which accounts require immediate attention and action to control. Obtaining the necessary information for analysis can be accomplished in a number of ways, including:

- Personal observations of daily departmental operations by the Dealer principal.
- Printing schedules of individual expense accounts (easily done with today's computer systems). The schedules will list the items that went into each expense total. If the schedules don't provide enough detail, they will identify which journals or source documents to look at for further information.

For example: the Miscellaneous account is over forecast, and after review of that account schedule, it shows a charge you are unaware of. The schedule indicates the source which is then checked to identify the item of expense that may have caused the account to exceed forecast.

Fundamentals of the analysis include:

- Directing that all incoming mail be opened by the Dealer. This will keep him or her informed on all departmental business, particularly incoming bills (accounts payables).
- Manager meetings to review budget limits and to evaluate expense control problems and solutions in detail

- Monthly recaps of expense accounts detailing the items in the second bullet above. Due to the time and expense involved in making these recaps, they should be limited to:
    - Expense accounts that show an unusual degree of change, or an absence of expected change
    - Expense accounts that are over forecast
    - Expense accounts that have historically proven to be difficult to keep under control

Planning

Establish an action plan for the expenses that are in need of special attention and control. It would be advisable for the Dealer, in conjunction with the appropriate manager, to meet first about the expense, then discuss the details of a final plan of action. It is important to understand that it would not be wise for the Dealer to establish a plan without first consulting with the effected manager. It is very possible that the manager could have a sound, business reason for a particular account's out-of-line condition. However. the final plan might have to include an expense account budget limitation, requiring the Dealer's approval for overages.

Policies

Established written policies should be made on each expense so problems can be resolved without dispute. Policies should include a report of problems that arise from the policy. This will allow corrections to be made if needed. Examples of policies might include Dealer approval for overages on expense account budgets, and limits on capital expenditures.

Assignment

No expense control program will succeed if specific individuals are not given the authority and responsibility for carrying out the actions necessary to control the expense in question.

Evaluation

If management does not undertake expense control procedures on a regular basis, "drifts" are likely to occur, resulting in increased expenses. Managers should be evaluated individually and advised at department manager meetings regarding their progress in keeping expenses within budget limits. Critical expenses should also be included in the Daily Operating Control. If the situation is severe, daily review might be necessary.

Other Analysis Issues

An important aspect of analyzing an expense is that the true cost of an expense is often not just the price paid for a specific item or service. For example: the sales manager decides to run a multi-day tent sale. In planning, budgets are estimated, approved, and set aside for the promotion. The estimates would typically include costs for advertising and promotion, supplies, refreshments, entertainment and tent rental. What is often forgotten in the budget estimating process are the other indirect costs that will be associated with the event. These "hidden costs" might include overtime pay for get-ready personnel to wash and move vehicles, salaries for clerical staff required to do extra billing or added receptionist coverage, or other unanticipated costs.

Another example might include: the expense of implementing a direct mail promotion. This promotion incurs direct costs for printing and postage, and possibly the purchase of a mailing list. The indirect, or "hidden" costs might include storage or employees' time to assemble and mail the pieces. All of these are indirect costs that add to the total cost of implementing a direct mail campaign. A current shortage of office help could be another indirect cost factor. Will this effort reduce the productive hours spent on other Dealership activities? All factors and "hidden costs" should be weighed against the potential value when judging the total outlay against these and other types of expenditures.

A cost-benefits analysis, or return on investment (ROI) analysis should include an evaluation of all possible expenses. These should be measured by cost versus projected sales return. However, an added problem is usually present. Unless the Dealer or departmental managers have had prior experience with an alternative approach, extra efforts may be needed to determine the likely costs and resulting benefits through increased sales.

In many expense categories, alternatives may be of questionable value. Example: Independent suppliers (outside services) may be needed for building and lot maintenance, lawn care, security, insurance, legal, reconditioning of used vehicles, data processing, payroll, advertising, etc. The lowest cost, doesn't always ensure acceptable value for the product or service received. Similarly, highest costs don't always translate to the greatest possible value. Therefore, special evaluation must take place regarding price **and** the value of the product or service that is being provided. An alternative that does not offer a materially better, cost-benefit result than the current expense item is not likely worthwhile.

Certain expenses, such as most taxes, have few alternatives and are not directly controllable by management. For others, there are no suitable alternative for the expenses. The supply of electricity or natural gas are usually examples of these types of items. The salary paid an inactive owner is sometimes another.

Expense Control - Individual Accounts

As mentioned previously, the heart of any expense control effort is the establishment of policies, systems and methods to control expenses. Of course methods vary, depending on the expense involved. However, review of all dealership accounts is essential to a timely and effective application of expense control. The following addresses some of the methods for control of individual expense accounts:

Variable Expense Control

While the business manager's major function is to control and/or reduce total expenses, contemplated action in the variable expense group must always be influenced by its immediate and future effect on the sale of new and used vehicles. For some business managers, particularly those with accounting backgrounds, envisioning a material benefit can sometimes be clouded by the expense realized or anticipated. They may not necessarily understand the impact an expense has on the sales and resulting gross profit that expense may generate. An example might include the implementation of a special sales contest. The expense of this contest might seem unreasonable to the business manager. However, if the contest generates additional sales, those expenses would be offset by the increase in gross and net profit.

Variable expenditures relate directly to new and used vehicle sales. Following a comparison and analysis of each expense account, along with an evaluation of current market penetration, sound judgment and progressive plans for maximum sales and gross profit might identify a controlled budget increase.

The following discussion on expenses has been tailored for the example statement. This procedure was used to illustrate again the distinction between form and substance in the financial statement.

Compensation - Vehicle Salespeople

Compensation for vehicle salespeople is comprised of the amount of all salaries, selling commissions and other compensation earned by car and truck salespeople on the sale of new or used units, plus amounts earned through the sale of accessories and other equipment installed on new units.

To effect control, the business manager and the Dealer should first review the dealership's compensation plan. The compensation plan should motivate salespeople to peak performance and achievement of better-than-average sales performance. That performance should include sales volume and gross profit, along with profit from the sale of aftermarket products and services. The review of the pay plan must also consider local competition. Successful managers have recognized that various compensation plans inspire varying degrees of motivation. They also know that most salespeople are motivated to higher levels of achievement by a higher compensation rate for above-average sales volume. Consideration should be given to paying a proportionately higher rate for sales or gross profit produced in excess of average sales accomplishments.

Pay plans based solely on volume and gross measurements can induce salespeople to sacrifice customer satisfaction for greater sales volume and higher grosses. Many of today's dealerships address this problem by incorporating Customer Satisfaction Index (CSI) performance criteria into their bonus plans. Under these compensation plans, salespeople must adhere to and maintain a minimum level of customer satisfaction in order to qualify for any volume or gross bonus.

The phenomenon of placing greater emphasis on CSI combined with new developments such as one price selling are causing a significant impact on compensation plans. Some dealerships have gone to straight salaries, with nominal bonuses for volume, gross and CSI performance. In those instances, the salary is roughly 80% to 90% of the total compensation. While this method of compensation is somewhat controversial, it is being implemented with reasonable success.

Because compensation plans are highly sensitive issues, any changes in the acknowledged compensation system should be put in writing and thoroughly discussed with each salesperson. Mutual agreement, in the form of a written plan, should also be formally acknowledged by both the salesperson and the manager. Historically, many dealership changed pay plans frequently, often to maximize short-term net profits. Short-term results often are high turnover and low morale. These short sighted management actions frequently contributed to lower long-term profitability.

Floor Plan Interest

Floor Plan Interest is the charge incurred when borrowing for the purpose of securing a new vehicle inventory. For the majority of Dealers, the only controllable factor is the volume of the inventory. It is difficult to negotiate rates with flooring institutions. Not only can used unit rates be more expensive than new, but the flooring of used units can cause lending institutions to raise the rates on new units if the institution begins to question a dealership's liquidity. Flooring of used units should be **absolutely avoided**. If it is still necessary, it must be closely monitored.

The size and composition of the dealership's new inventory requires solid business judgment that must be made in light of prevailing market and interest rate conditions. Guidelines should be in place to govern inventory volume, and should be monitored monthly. Special attention should be paid to ensuring that sales management has been trained in effective ordering and inventory control.

Customer Relations Adjustments (Policy Work-Vehicles)

Policy work includes charges for labor and materials (at internal rates) expended on new and used cars previously sold by the dealership where neither the customer nor manufacturer will be charged. Because all new vehicles are covered by warranty, this expense account typically includes policy expenses resulting from used vehicle sales.

Adjustments are usually initiated by a customer complaint and are incurred through expenses accrued in satisfying that owner. To bring these expenses into line, the business manager and Dealer need to question and review the dealership procedure for reviewing owner complaints. They can then determine who has the authority for approval. For control, a definite procedure should be established, and authority delegated to the appropriate manager(s). The causes of complaints should be reviewed periodically and action taken to improve vehicle prep and reconditioning procedures.

Advertising

The expense for advertising purchased by the dealership includes the costs of newspaper, radio, television, direct mail (including postage), window posters, painted signs, billboards, telephone directory ads, hand bills, promotional materials, service letters, handout novelties, sponsorship of athletic teams or events, Dealer group advertising, free lubrications, etc.

Promotional expense strongly influence sales and gross profit. Therefore, advertising expenditures should be carefully planned and evaluated to ensure maximum effectiveness. Department managers should assist in preparing all advertising on behalf of their departments, and should retain approval authority. There should also be a plan in place for periodic measurement of audience coverage and advertising effectiveness through business reply cards (BRCs), giveaways or other measurable incentive fulfillment activities.

Advertising expense controls should take into account the following questions: Are cars held in stock so long that they are responsible for unnecessary advertising expense? Is a definite advertising budget provided each month that is allocated to each department? Are the actual expenditures in each department checked against the budget after the close of the month? Is advertising copy approved by the management of the dealership? Does the dealership regularly review it's advertising contracts with reference to the most advantageous rate? Does the type of advertising used produce results?

Demo Expense

Demo Expense encompasses all expenses relative to the operation and maintenance of new vehicles in demonstrator service, including repair damage. It should be remembered, in addition to gasoline and oil, license plates, insurance, maintenance, inspections and all related charges are also charged to this account.

A cost benefit analysis should be made including the all costs before a vehicle is placed in demo service. Periodically, the use of each and every unit should be justified by the same criteria. Because of the high cost of offering demonstrators and insurance liability, most dealership have either eliminated demonstrators altogether or charge the user for the privilege. Many Dealers still provide demonstrators to managers as a fringe benefit. Some Dealers will charge the manager for the benefit, while others don't.

Special caution should be taken to remain within IRS regulations governing tax code treatment of demonstrators. The IRS treats the value of a demonstrator as taxable income. Therefore, the dealership must place a reasonable value on the use of the demonstrator, then withhold income tax based on that value. A CPA should be consulted for specific rules and guidelines.

Vehicle Maintenance Expense

Vehicle Maintenance Expense is the cost of maintaining units in inventory once they have been placed in a salable condition. Because of the importance of turning inventory, and the high interest cost associated with inventories, this account is especially important. It is vital that all units be properly maintained (washed). Appearance is a critical factor in helping to clinch a sale.

Fixed Overhead Expense Control

Fixed overhead expenses, resulting from the staffing, operation and maintenance of the dealership, directly support the departmental organization. Because of their varied nature, and the fact that they directly support the revenue producing departments, each should be carefully considered and budgeted, and it's direct control pinpointed as the responsibility of specific dealership supervisory personnel.

Salaries - Owners

All compensation, excluding bonuses, of the bona fide owner or owners of the business, and any inactive firm members, is included under the owners' salaries account. This expense is directly controllable. The Dealer's salary should be set at a similar level to an executive of a comparable profit-producing business.

Key question to consider when establishing controls include: Would as much be paid to a general manager to do the same job? Are salaries paid to inactive firm members? Is any bonus paid only from profit?

Salaries - Supervision

This category is the total of all compensation for dealership managers. Similar to that of salespeople, manager compensation plans should provide the incentive to produce acceptable sales, gross profit and net profit levels. It should also include provisions for CSI performance. Compensation plans for managers vary greatly from dealership to dealership. Generally, the one thing they have in common is some type of bonus structure tied to net profit. If the manager is paid a bonus on sales or gross profit, but not net profit, there is little incentive to make expense control a top priority.

To encourage team effort between all managers within the dealership, consideration should be given to implementing a special bonus for overall dealership profitability. Because a sales manager can't control the expenses of the service department, this bonus should be an extra incentive. However, managers are often in a position to help support the sales efforts of all departments.

Salaries-Clerical

Accountants, bookkeepers, cashiers, telephone receptionists, billing clerks, payroll clerks, accounts payable and receivable persons, and other clerical employees are included within the Salaries-Clerical account. The administration of today's automobile business, with its complex structure, requires well-organized internal processes and procedures, which in turn may necessitate a large clerical staff.

Questions to consider include: Do outside duties or poor management create the need for excessive clerical staff? Can clerical staff headcount be reallocating responsibilities, creating more equal distribution of the work? Would the physical relocation of personnel performing clerical work help to reduce lost time? Does the clerical staff have the proper equipment (computers, software, calculators, typewriters, etc.) to efficiently perform their jobs?

To help control Salaries - Clerical expenses, consideration should be given to: Are there excessive numbers of notes and accounts receivable outstanding that require additional time and effort to post, handle receipts and follow-up collections? Is accurate and uniform accounting information received on or before the tenth of each month? Do other departments cooperate in turning in reports, particularly at the end of the month?

Other Salaries and Wages

The earnings of personnel such as watchpersons, janitors, general porters and others fall within this category. Nonproductive (non revenue-producing) employees must be limited to the minimum number necessary to ensure efficient operations. To avoid overstaffing, a list of employees and their respective duties should be made. This list should be carefully reviewed and responsibilities combined, wherever possible. Savings may be effected by reallocating of responsibilities or developing new procedures

Absentee Wages - Productive Personnel

Absentee wages are those covering vacation, holiday, and sick leave pay. They also include wages paid for time spent by productive service personnel attending training. Charging non- productive costs to this account provides a better measure of the profit efficiency of the service department and is a necessity for a cost benefit analysis.

Taxes - Payroll

This account contains a monthly provision for the employees' share of F.I.C.A., state and federal unemployment, and other payroll taxes, with the exception of Workmen's Compensation, which is usually accounted for under the employee benefits or insurance-other categories. Legal requirements limit control largely to the number and compensation rate of employees on the payroll.

Employee Benefits

This account would include the amount of contribution by the dealership to employee benefit plans, such as group life insurance, medical or dental insurance. The Dealer should consider various flexible benefit plans. The needs of today's employees are vastly different from those of the past, resulting in highly varied benefit requirements. Once these benefit policies are established, control is limited to the number of participants. In assessing the worth of the benefits, consideration should be given to their value and effect on employee morale. High morale provides greater employee loyalty with resultant profit-producing effects. Great care must be utilized when selecting various benefit providers, particularly medical insurance carriers. It is often prudent to hire the services of a specialist in employee benefits. Reviewing all the policy provisions and exclusions, along with assessing rates can be extremely confusing and time consuming.

Workmen's Compensation

Workmen's Compensation is an insurance that protects the dealership employee from lost wages caused by on-the-job injury. If an employee is injured at the dealership, resulting in a lengthy absence, wages are covered under this insurance.

The direct cost of premiums is based on the number of employees, total payroll and claims history. Therefore, policies, procedures and training can help reduce claims by making the workplace safer. This should be a top priority of the dealership management, and should be a never-ending process. All too often, dealerships fail to have established safety regulations or become lax in enforcing them. One serious injury is generally all it takes to wake up management.

As mentioned, business managers differ on the placement of this expense. It may be found under employee benefits or insurance-other under the fixed expense heading.

Pension Fund

The pension fund is the provision for the employer's contribution to employee plans for retirement, pension, or annuities. Most common are 401K programs. Although rare, it also includes the compensation paid retired employees in lieu of a formal pension plan. Traditionally, once these policies and programs were set up, control was limited to the number of participants. In a depressed market, Dealers learn that everything is negotiable. This account must be reviewed with legal counsel. Competitive and social trends, along with morale issues should be considered when the pension fund is evaluated.

Company Car Expense

Company vehicle expenses are those incurred in the operation, repair, and upkeep of all company owned vehicles excluding demonstrators. These include courtesy vehicles, service cars, wreckers, parts delivery trucks, collectors' cars, driver training cars and other vehicles used for general purposes. Lease and rental units are not included in this account.

Control can be achieved by excluding vehicles not used directly in company business such as family vehicles, and also by reducing the number of company vehicles to the minimum necessary without impairing operating efficiency. Drivers permanently assigned company vehicles should be held responsible for their maintenance and upkeep of these vehicles.

Are expenses of vehicles owned and used personally by individuals in this account?

Office Supplies

This account consists of the cost of all stationary and office supplies used in the business, such as bookkeeping supplies, letterheads, envelopes, pens and pencils, repair orders, invoices, counter tickets, etc.

Consideration should be given to: Is an authorized purchase order used to secure material? Are all orders approved by one person? Are purchases made in sufficient quantities to obtain the best possible price? Are supplies secured for protection against loss, damage or theft? If expenditures are extensive, are charges listed and reviewed individually?

Other Supplies

The cost of all supplies other than office supplies purchased for use in the business are included in the other supplies account. Small tools, sweeping compound, solvents, grease, brooms, mops, rags, chamois, light bulbs, cotter pins, graphite, drinking cups, etc., are examples of other supplies. Body Shop paint materials should not be charged to this account.

The many items included here require careful organization for their control. Purchases should be made in practical quantities within an allotted budget, and supplies should be inventoried each month as a guide for purchasing. A nominal charge should be placed on customer-pay repair order charges for shop supplies.

Question to ask include: Is an effort made to secure the lowest price for services and supplies? How is this done, by whom and when? Does one person authorize the purchase of all supplies? Are supplies protected against damage, loss, or pilferage?

Uniform and Laundry Expense

The cost of employees' uniforms and laundry paid for by the dealership is included in this account.   In some dealerships, this cost is absorbed as a benefit to the employee. In others, the total cost is charged back to employees. Some Dealers or managers may opt to charge a portion of the cost to affected employees.

Contributions

This account covers all donations or contributions to religious, educational, or charitable groups, etc. Control can be effected by having all requests for contributions referred to one individual, usually the Dealer. Automobile dealerships are frequent targets for charitable solicitations, and can hardly afford to accommodate every request. Care must be exercised to avoid the negative publicity that might result from turning a charity down. Set policies can help lessen negative feelings about being turned down. They will also inform employees about which charities the dealership is willing to support.

Outside Services

Expenses for protection service, service for bookkeeping or inventory, carpet cleaning service, collection agency fees, credit reports, window washing, management fees, etc., are accounted for under outside services. Expenditures for such services can be controlled by authorizing one person to make the purchase of these services and by evaluating whether each service provides sufficient benefit to the dealership in light of the cost.

Travel and Entertainment

The total expense of travel and entertainment for business purposes includes the traveling and subsistence expenses of dealership personnel a "on the road," customer entertainment, traveling to auctions, etc. This expense is directly controllable by the Dealer. All charges should be supported by an itemized, paid and receipted bill, and should be reimbursed only after each is submitted, reviewed and approved.

The IRS has very specific rules regarding entertainment expenses. Basically, only 20% of total entertainment expenses are deductible as a business expense. Therefore, entertainment should be kept to a minimum, and should be used only with those who are important customers or suppliers to the dealership.

Questions that should be considered include: Is each item actually necessary? Is every item applicable to the business? Is each item supported by an itemized invoice? Is the account actually analyzed every month?

Membership, Dues and Publications

All charges for membership, dues in business organizations, subscriptions for business and commercial magazines and papers, etc., are recorded within this account. These expenditures can be controlled by discontinuing subscriptions and memberships which do not sufficiently benefit the business, by checking with each department manager to determine if trade journals, pricing guides, shop manuals, etc., are being used, by avoiding automatic renewals, and by reviewing periodically a listing of all charges made to this account.

There are certain membership dues identified by the IRS as non-deductible business expenses. The advice of a CPA should be sought for clarification.

Legal and Audit

Legal and Auditing are those expenses for legal and accounting services, retainer or individual case charges paid to attorneys, auditors, and collection agencies. It also includes costs for recording mortgages, bills of sale (building and land), transfers, court costs, etc. If an attorney or auditing firm is on a retainer, the dealership should determine whether the benefits justify the expense. Accurate and uniform accounting can minimize the need for frequent auditing services.

Would a newer, more efficient computer system provide faster, more accurate accounting, thus reducing the audit expenses? Is the dealership being unnecessarily exposed to litigation through carelessness?

Telephone

Telephones are critical to the day-to-day operations of an automobile dealership, and are a significant expense. It is also an expense that is commonly abused. All telephone and fax (facsimile) charges to the dealership should be carefully controlled to avoid excessive expense.

Consideration should be given to: Are salespersons effective at selling from stock, avoiding frequent long distance calls locating vehicles? Is there a policy statement regarding personal usage? Are all long distance calls authorized? Have other long-distance carriers been investigated, including utilization of toll-free numbers? Are charges for directory assistance high?

The phone company, by request, will monitor telephone activity for a period, and reveal waste in phone use and will see if the dealership's equipment should be updated.

Training Expense

The expense of training employees includes training school tuition, salesperson training materials, in-dealership training seminar fees, educational films and materials and meals, lodging and transportation while attending training schools. To control training expenses, each requisition for the purchase of any program should be signed by the department manager and approved by the Dealer only after a cost benefit analysis.

Data Processing Expense

All computer and related expenses are included in this account. It will also include outside data processing costs such as payroll processing.

Policy Work-Parts and Service

This heading is often referred to as repair comebacks. In a theoretical situation it would be the responsibility of the technician for his own work, but this is not always practical. In such situations, not only must the amounts be closely watched, but the customer must be followed up to make sure that the work is redone to his or her satisfaction.

High levels of comebacks may indicate productivity problems with a particular technician, identify a training need, uncover specific tool requirements, or demonstrate a need for employment termination.

Transportation and Freight

This account covers expenses incurred for freight, express, cartage and postage for the shipment of parts, accessories, body and paint materials and other inventory items to and from the dealership. The parts manager is directly responsible for controlling this expense.

Manufacturers generally pay for shipment of stock order parts. Additional charges occur when special or emergency orders are placed. The parts manager should be thoroughly aware of all parts ordering policies that affect who is responsible for shipping.

Miscellaneous Expense

Wide open to interpretation, and sometimes abuse, the Miscellaneous Expense account becomes the bucket in which to place all other expenses that do not have clearly identifiable accounts already established. Because this account can be abused, it should be held to a minimum and analyzed by the business manager for items which should have been charged to a more appropriate account. It may also show some items which were incurred without the Dealer's knowledge.

Are the items charged to this account analyzed each month? Are any items listed that are not essential to sales and profits? Are department managers consulted frequently in an effort to reduce the amount and number of charges? Remember, little leaks sink big ships.

Special Expense Considerations

There is one other important area of expense control that is **not** always accounted for on the profit and loss statement: Invalid Claim Expense ("charge-backs") and Factory Receivables - Other

<u>Invalid Claim Expense</u>

In the trade, normally termed "warranty rejects" are warranty claims refused by the manufacturer. These amounts are usually accounted for in the factory receivable account on the balance sheet. Not only is the service manager responsible for reviewing each refused claim, but management must be kept aware of all unpaid claims outstanding with the factory. Most manufacturers have specific policies regarding the length of time allowed for clearing up any disputes.

Fixed Expense (Including Occupancy)

These accounts are not discussed individually because of the length of time it normally takes to effect change. Once a lease is signed or a depreciation schedule has been established, the dealership is "locked-in" for a specified period of time. This does not remove the responsibility of conducting periodic follow-ups to take advantage of profitable changes in IRS depreciation allowances or other financial guidelines. Before establishing depreciation schedules, the advice of a CPA, particularly one familiar with dealership operations, should be sought.

Although utilities, equipment and repair accounts are included in this section, they are somewhat controllable. These expenses vary significantly for each individual dealership and business situation, emphasizing the point that the Dealer must be aware of what these costs are, and must ensure that controls are in place to help keep them to a minimum.

Rent and Rent Equivalent

Each dealership has either rent expenses or other expenses termed "rent equivalents." The classification depends on whether the land and building facilities used in the business are leased or owned by the dealership. When the facilities are leased, the expenses will be rent and amortization - leaseholds. Rent is all payments for rental of land and buildings used in the business. The account, amortization - leaseholds, applies to the monthly pro-rata charge-off of capital investments made to acquire leaseholds and to effect improvements in lease facilities, such as new buildings and paving of lot surfaces on leased lands. When the facilities are owned, the expenses will be repairs - real estate, depreciation - buildings and improvements, taxes - real estate, and insurance - buildings and improvements.

Regardless of whether the land and buildings are leased or owned, the rent or rent equivalent should be consistent with the real value of the property and its worth as a market place of profit-producing sales.

SUMMARY

Consideration of the future is necessary to every business. It involves the continuous process of planning for results and then controlling to obtain those results. Many small firms that operate on a day-to-day basis with very little planning find themselves out of business. They pay too much attention to the problems at hand, ignoring the more serious issues of the future.

Planning requires goals and objectives. A plan without a goal is like taking a trip with no clear destination in mind. In business, the main objective is to make a satisfactory return on investment, and to build a satisfied owner base. Budgets and forecasts define goals and objectives in dollars. Therefore, they are important tools for profit-planning.

Sales and profit forecasts, expense budgets, planning, directing, and controlling are the necessary ingredients for maximizing profits. They include estimates for all major items that affect gross profits, sales, purchases, inventories, and expenses. They should reflect both the long-range and short-range goals that the Dealer seeks to attain. As with most forecasts, the budget should be made annually and reviewed and revised on a monthly basis.

Every budget is based on the dealership's departmentalized accounting system. Therefore, it is essential that expense items be charged to the correct accounts and distributed to the appropriate departments. This will facilitate the most effective control because management can then delegate expense control responsibility in specific dollar amounts to each of the department managers.

Before preparing the budgets, the actual and budgeted figures from prior months should be compared and analyzed. This is the same type of performance review that is made before developing the sales and profit forecasts.

After the budget is prepared, the work of control cannot be limited to monthly reviews. Experienced department managers who are familiar with their departmental data of sales, grosses, and expenses develop a sense of awareness of their day-to-day position.

In addition, a department manager should personally participate in developing the department's budget, because it provides a strong incentive to keep the expenses within the budget limits and prove that judgment was correct when the expense projection was made.

The Dealer and business manager are responsible for monitoring the budgets, which also helps make them more effective. In their observations of the current operations, they can recognize adverse trends and remind the department manager of the budget commitments. For example, if the service manager wants to hire several marginally capable technicians' helpers, he must realize that the resulting increase in his fringe benefit expenses may cause him to exceed his budget limits and affect his operating profit. If the parts manager wants to add a parts van for a counterperson to sell from along a wholesale route, he must realize that the increase in company car expense may cause him to exceed his budget, unless the expected increase in sales and profitability will justify the added expense.

Thus, between the expense insight which department managers develop and management's daily monitoring of departmental operations, expense budgets can be controlled.

Automotive retailing is a very dynamic business and, as such, flexible budgets should be used which provide alternative expense limits so a Dealer can adapt quickly when market change occurs. To understand and use a flexible budget, management must recognize how variable, semi-fixed and fixed expenses relate to sales volume. Volume directly affects only variable expenses, while it indirectly affects personnel and semi-fixed expenses. The effect of volume (if any, during the short term) on fixed expenses is also indirect. Variable, personnel and semi-fixed expenses require flexible budgets because their estimates are connected with changes in the sales volume. The flexible budget is geared to various sales levels and is adjusted when actual conditions change. This budget presents more accurate estimates of variable, personnel and semi-fixed expenses than would a static budget. Expense estimates can be calculated for the forecasted volume by using the expense-per-unit-sold in recent past periods. The variable expense estimates can also be made at higher and lower levels of sales activity. When these estimates are made, a budget can be prepared showing these expenses at each of the sales levels for the affected departments.

Expenses that do not change directly with changes in volume can be controlled by a static budget. This budget is not calculated at different sales volume levels because it is not flexible with changes that may occur.

The only time to control expenses is before they occur and dollars are spent. By preparing budgets with as much care and foresight as possible, they become effective management tools for expense control.

CHAPTER 4

CHAPTER IV

RELATED FUNCTIONS

Credit Management

Not all credit sales originating in the dealership are installment sales for which a finance institution holds a contract. Installment financing is designed for the retail customer who must spread payment over a period of time, generally ranging from one to four or more years, simply because the purchase requires a substantial amount of money. Thus, installment financing is fairly well limited to the sale of new or used cars and trucks, and will be discussed in Chapter VI -- Retail Financing.

The Dealer does have many other credit customers who make purchases that do not require payments that extend over a long period of time. These customers simply charge their purchases and pay for them when billed. The usual cycle is thirty days from charge to payment. In certain situations a cash discount, normally not to exceed 2%, is allowed for early payment of wholesale accounts. Most wholesale parts customers, as an example, operate on such a basis. For most dealerships, charge accounts are limited to local businesses. The growth and acceptance of consumer credit cards such as Master Card, VISA, American Express and others has minimized the need for individual consumer charge accounts.

It is generally accepted that the extension of credit is a necessary part of doing business today, and those businesses that do not extend credit would find it difficult to remain competitive with those who do. Therefore, the point is not whether a dealership should or should not make credit available to its customers, credit extension is a necessity, and the dealership must establish and maintain prudent credit and collection policies to safeguard itself from over-extending credit and ultimately losses due to uncollectable debts. Responsibility for establishing and enforcing credit policies usually lies with the dealership's business manager.

In establishing dealership credit policy, the first factor to carefully consider is the extent to which the dealership is in a position to carry receivables in total. **Extreme caution** must be exercised to ensure that operating capital is not excessively tied up in receivables, creating a cash flow problem. The minimum cash on hand (or otherwise available) should be equivalent to at least one full month's total dealership expenses, plus any other cash requirement. A thirty-day period theoretically represents the average elapsed time between a credit sale and payment.

Past due receivables do not normally become total losses. Nevertheless, there is some loss of net profit. If the Dealer has too many past due receivables, operating capital may shrink to the point where money must be borrowed to pay operating expenses. The interest on such loans will naturally cut into net profit. If excessive follow-up is required to effect collection, an added expense is incurred which also diminishes the profit from the sale. If an attorney or collection agency must be employed as a last resort, the expenses can become considerable. Finally, at least some past due accounts tend to become uncollectable and, of course, in such instances a total loss results.

There is no shortcut to good credit and collections. It is only through strict adherence to sound principles and practices that credit can be extended safely. The lack of policies and procedures leads to heavy losses from worthless accounts and serious impairment of capital. The following table lists reasons for excessive receivables and recurring bad debts.

Excessive Receivables and Bad Debts

I.   Poor Quality Credit Extension
- No one person responsible for extending credit
- Inexperienced person granting credit
- Poor investigative procedures
- Appropriate terms and limits not established
- Maximum dealership credit line extended

II.   Poor Quality Collection Program
- No one person responsible for collection
- Inexperienced person in charge of collection
- Customers not billed in time to meet due date
- Too lenient with past due accounts
- No consistent effort on difficult accounts
- Monthly statements inaccurate
- Worthless accounts not charged off promptly

Past due receivables cost the Dealer money because they:

- Cause the loss of the earning power from money that is tied up
- Necessitate borrowing and consequent interest payments
- Add costs of collection for accounts which frequently prove uncollectable
- Ultimately past due receivables cause the loss of both profit and capital involved in the original sale

To maximize profits resulting from credit sales, and minimize losses incurred as a result of the sale, rigid controls must be established. There are four basic fundamentals that will then enable a Dealer to maintain practical control of credit extension: (1) one person should be responsible for credit extension, (2) there should be adequate credit history investigation on all new customers, (3) definite terms and limits for each customer should be established and rigidly adhered to and (4) total dealership credit line should not be exceeded.

Responsibility

The first fundamental requirement is that credit be extended only to those customers who, either through past dealings with the business or after reasonable investigation, appear to have the ability and willingness to pay obligations promptly when due. The person charged with responsibility for extending credit should establish a credit file of customers who meet these qualifications. The names placed in this file can come from two sources: established customers and new customers. The names of established customers, who in the past have paid their bills promptly, as evidenced by the accounts and notes receivables summary schedules, and who are still considered good credit risks, should be placed in the credit file.

Credit Application

In evaluating a prospective customer for a credit line, investigation of the applicant must be made. Potential credit risk must be minimized. A credit application should be filled out for every new customer and placed in the credit file. When properly filled out, it is an important key to qualifying new credit prospects. Due to rapidly changing laws, it is advised that an attorney be consulted regarding the credit form that is to be used. A sample credit application is shown on the following page. If the application is from a business, those authorized to use the company charge account should also be listed.

Terms and Limits

The third basic credit fundamental is to set up definite terms for and limits on each customer's account. This will help assure that the individual customer's credit limit is held within reasonable bounds. These limits are generally a flat dollar amount such as the account balance not to exceed $3,000.

Dealership Credit Line

The fourth basic fundamental is to hold the total dealership capital tied up in receivables to a specific amount. This total should not be exceeded. If growth of credit demand is evident then a new total dealership credit limit should be established at that time.

Since the financial condition, income, etc., of customers will vary greatly, it is evident that more credit can be extended safely to some than to others, even though the latter are good credit risks up to a certain point. This fact cannot be ignored if credit operations are to be conducted on a sound basis. Consequently a credit limit should be placed on each customer's credit account and also on the ledger sheet to avoid the possibility of a customer obtaining more credit than allowed.

To generate mutual agreement on credit limits, always identify the precise amount of credit available to the customer at the time they are approved. If this is done diplomatically, it will serve to dispel any feeling a customer may have that the limit is either too low or totally unnecessary in his or her case.

Internal Control

In order to avoid the possible over-extension of credit, a procedure for internal control should be established. It is recommended in a vehicle service situation that the customer be given an estimate of all work to be performed. (This is required by law in most states). The office copy should be used to verify credit limits. In such a case, the customer and the Dealer know not only the total of the bill but how it is to be paid.

In order to avoid the possibility of an over-extension of credit on parts sales, it is necessary that all charge invoices be posted to the accounts receivable ledger daily. The individual responsible for posting this ledger should immediately notify the business manager when the current balance is equals to or exceeds the credit limit. If the volume is such that the credit limit appears to be inadequate, the business manager must decide if further credit should be extended or possibly withdrawn. Whatever action is taken the copy of the credit card on file in the parts department should be revised and the revision called to the attention of the parts manager.

APPLICATION FOR CREDIT

PLEASE TYPE OR PRINT   Date of Application _______________________

Name of Firm ____

Address ____

City, State, Zip Code ____

Telephone (   )___________________   FAX Number (   ) _______________

Years in Business ___________________   State of Incorporation_______________

Type of Business: (   ) Corporation   (   ) Partnership   (   ) Propietorship

Names, Titles Of All Principals:

| **NAME** | **TITLE** |

1. ____

2. ____

3. ____

Exempt From Sales Tax: (   ) NO   (   ) YES What is Your Tax Exemption Number _______________

Contact or Authorized Buyer ___________________________________

Number of Employees _______________   Estimated Purchase Volume $ _______________

Do You Require Purchase Order Numbers? (   ) YES   (   ) NO

TRADE REFERENCES:

Name_______________________   Name_______________________

Address____________________   Address____________________

City, State, Zip ____________   City, State, Zip ____________

Phone No. (   ) ____________   Phone No. (   ) ____________

DUN & BRADSTREET NO. ____________   PARENT COMPANY? (   )YES (   ) NO

BANK REFERENCE:

Name_______________________   Account Number _______________

Address____________________   Phone Number _______________

City, State, Zip ____________   Bank Officer's Name _______________

CREDIT TERMS AND GUARANTEE:

The applicant agrees to the following terms:
1. To pay in full all invoices within 30 days.
2. If the Total Balance Due is not paid within that time, then a finance charge of 1.5% will be imposed on the balance past due as shown on the subsequent monthly statement and customer agrees to pay the finance charge.
3. Miles Fox Company may limit or cancel all charge privileges if a Past Due Balance is shown on the account or there is reason to believe the account will not be paid as it becomes due.
4. In the event the applicant fails to pay when due, he agrees to pay all costs of collection including reasonable attorney fees.
5. The applicant states that the information included in this credit application is factual to the best of his knowledge. The applicant hereby authorizes Miles Fox Company to investigate his credit record and to verify statements made herein.
6. To induce Miles Fox Company to extend credit, the above applicant guarantees payment, when due, of all amounts, including finance charges payable to Miles Fox Company. Revocation of this agreement shall not affect the guarantee with respect to amounts owed before receipt of revocation. Without notice to applicant, Miles Fox Company may: 1. Change the time or manner of payment of debts. 2. Change the rate of interest. If the applicant fails to pay the account when due, Miles Fox Company may proceed here under, without prior notice, with suit against the applicant for payment.

Firm ____

Authorized Signature _______________________________

Printed Name _______________________________________

Collections

It is imperative that a delinquent receivables collection procedure be established. This should entail the following:

- Either a delinquent collection notice or a delinquent credit collection letter must be mailed to the account three days after due date.
- Delinquent collection notices (generally up to four) or letters must be mailed to the account each five days until the final notice or letter.
- If the account becomes 30 days past due, personal follow-up becomes necessary. This follow-up is done by the person who extended the credit originally or someone in the dealership who knows the account personally, i.e., the department manager, Dealer, or possibly some other supervisory person. This should first take the form of a phone call, and if no satisfactory results ensues, a personal visit. Diplomacy must be used in handling these contacts. Dealers do not want to lose a good customer. There are times when small businesses have cash flow problems, or a temporary illness may cause a delay in payment. However, there is nothing wrong with asking for the money that is owed - the Dealer needs what is coming in order to stay in business.
- All efforts must be exhausted before the account is turned over to an attorney or collection agency. This includes a letter from the dealership or possibly their attorney as the final written notice that legal action may be taken to collect. While it is the usual practice to write off a debt over 90 days past due from an accounting point of view, this does not stop the collection follow-up in person or by phone. When it appears fruitless to follow any further, the final action might be small claims court, through an attorney or possibly a collection agency. If a collection agency is utilized, they will most likely charge half of whatever dollar amount they obtain from the delinquent account.

Following below are samples of collection notices. They are in sequence, ranging from a gentle reminder to a firm request - in keeping with the step-by-step collection procedure.

<table>
<tr><td>

A Payment on Your Account is Overdue

A friendly reminder that according to the terms of your charge account a payment of $______________
was due ______________

If payment has been made, please disregard this notice.

</td><td>

PAYMENT OVERDUE

For the Second Time we call your attention to the payment on your account, overdue since
____
Please take care of this at once.

If you have already sent your payment, please disregard this notice.

</td></tr>
</table>

FIRST   SECOND

A REMINDER OF YOUR PROMISE		FINAL NOTICE

<table>
<tr><td>

A REMINDER OF YOUR PROMISE

You promised we would receive a payment on your account on or before_________________
We have not yet received the payment, neither have we heard from you.

Please give this your immediate attention.

</td><td>

FINAL NOTICE

It is necessary that we see you or hear from you without further delay regarding your payment, overdue since___________________

</td></tr>
<tr><td align="center">**THIRD**</td><td align="center">**FOURTH**</td></tr>
</table>

Collection Stickers

The same effect can be achieved by affixing gummed stickers, with similar messages, to the customer's statements.

The following are sample collection letters which might be mailed at 5- to 10-day intervals in place of collection notices to motivate past due customers to pay. The tone of such letters is important. The early reminders should be phrased in such a way that the customer is not offended by the request. (The customer may have forgotten, may have had every intention to pay or may have received poor service which needs to be cleared up first.

The final notice needs to be firm, but must still leave the door open for the customer to make the payment on his own.

<table>
<tr><td>

Dear:

Our records show that your account is past due.

May we have your remittance promptly or your comments regarding any possible inaccuracy in your account?
A duplicate statement is attached for your convenience.

Sincerely,

P.S. Please disregard this notice if payment is in the mail.

</td><td>

FIRST NOTICE

</td></tr>
</table>

<table>
<tr><td>

SECOND NOTICE

</td><td>

Dear:

We have not yet received your remittance for your account balance of $_____________, which has been past due since______________.

It is not our intent to be overly insistent about this account, however, if there is a problem concerning payment, we need to be advised.

Thank you!

Sincerely,

</td></tr>
</table>

Dear:

We dislike annoying our customers about unpaid accounts, however, we can pay our own bills only by collecting what is owing to us.

Please remit at once or let us know when me may expect your payment.

Sinecerely,

THIRD NOTICE

The following types of collection letters may be mailed if the account has failed to respond. After the final notice, the types of actions described in the final letter should be undertaken. It may be desirable to specify a time period, such as 5 days after receipt, to establish a time for action to start on the final letter.

Dear:

Your account in the amount of $_______________ remains unpaid although we have sent you several statements and reminders regarding it.

Perhaps payment has been delayed because you do not find it convenient to take care of this entire amount immediately? If so, we will be glad to arrange for you to take advantage of our budget plan of payments. Small weekly payments can be arranged to suit your convenience.

Please forward remittance to cover your account, or stop in to discuss the matter with us.

Yours very truly,

FOURTH NOTICE

Dear:

Payment of your account in the amount of $___________ is long overdue.

You have not answered our previous letters requesting payment of this amount and consequently, it will be necessary to discontinue your charge privileges unless arrangements are made promptly to clear up this overdue debt.

If it is not convenient for you to clear up this matter in one payment, please contact us to arrange a time schedule covering payments on a monthly basis.

Sincerely,

FIFTH NOTICE

Dear:

Since you have not responded to our many letters regarding payment of your long overdue
account, it will be necessary to turn this matter over to our attorney for collecion.

Should this matter require litigation, we will seek to recover legal fees, court costs and interest in addition to
the amount which is owed on your account.

In order to avoid the above action, we suggest that you get in touch with us within 5 days and arrange for the
payment of $_______________.

Sincerely,

FINAL NOTICE.

Late Charges

All accounts receivable charge accounts should have a policy covering late charges or fees. Commonly,
interest is charged on any balance beyond 30-days. Some prefer to charge a flat amount for any late
payment. In either case, some charge should be made. After all, the dealership is not a bank. If the
dealership's funds are tied up due to late payments, they are then entitled to compensation for such
tardiness. *Before* any late fees or interest policies are established, an attorney should be consulted.
Every state has laws that govern the amount of interest or late fees that can be charged.

Responsibility

The first fundamental requirement of any sound, well-controlled collection procedure is that one person
in the organization be definitely charged with responsibility for follow-up and collection of past due
accounts and notes receivable. This will sometimes be the same individual who is charged with the
responsibility for extending credit.

Accounts Receivable Trial Balance

In the procedure, after statements have been mailed, an accounts receivable trial balance is prepared
showing the status of each account. Each account shows the total amount due, as well as how much of
the amount is current and how much, if any, is past due.

All past due accounts are classified on a 30-, 60-, or 90-day past due basis. In some accounting systems,
past due categories also include an over 90-day classification. Where special circumstances do not dictate
a deviation from established policy, 60- and 90-day past due accounts are marked for a special collection
follow-up procedure starting with a phone call or personal visit. A record of all follow-up calls, together
with the results of such calls are made on the accounts receivable trial balance, and placed in the
customer's file.

Immediate Effort

Once credit has been extended to a customer, a critical situation develops on the failure of that customer to pay his obligation when due. Experience shows ***beyond a doubt*** that the longer an account is past due the harder it is to collect. This is particularly important if the dealership has a business customer who has incurred a significant account balance, and there is some evidence of an impending bankruptcy situation. If legal action against the account holder is required, and it takes place before they file for bankruptcy, odds of collecting are greatly improved. Therefore, the first fundamental is that collection effort be started immediately after a receivable becomes past due, and that it be followed up persistently until paid or determined to be worthless. It is advisable to remember that a poor-paying customer is often made a good-paying customer by prompt collection action.

Consistent Effort

It is essential to a well-controlled collection effort that some means be available which will enable the Dealer to know the names of those customers who are delinquent in their payments, the amount of the delinquency and the progress being made in collecting past due obligations from month to month. The trial balance and collection follow-up sheet provide this necessary information.

Small Claims Court

Small claims court can be a very cost-effective means for aiding in the collection process, and should be considered whenever possible. Small claims courts allow the dealership, or anyone, to sue without the need of an attorney. In fact, attorneys are not permitted in most small claims courts. Additionally, these courts charge a nominal fee for the process, generally around $35-$100 depending on the case amount or local and state policies. Therefore, the person responsible for customer accounts receivables should become familiar with the small claims court in their area, and its processes and procedures.

Merchant Credit Cards

Most Dealers find that accepting credit cards (Master Card, VISA, American Express) increase the dollar value of the sale, and helps to attract new customers. More importantly, credit cards help to reduce the dealership's burden in credit and collection procedures. Collection on these accounts is over within a few days after the charge, since the dealership is credited for the amount by the bank. All that must done at the time of the purchase is to check to be sure that the card hasn't expired, that it isn't on a stop list, that the signature on the card and the sales slip are the same, and to obtain approval for the charge through a transaction authorization center. Most merchants use a swipe machine that reads a magnetic strip on the back of the credit card. The card is swiped through the machine, then the amount of the sale is entered. The machine then dials the authorization center via phone lineSeconds later, an approval code is displayed. All of this takes a minimum of time.

What the Dealer doesn't have to do (that would have to be done with their own charge accounts), is prepare, offer and process application forms for new accounts, investigate credit on applications, perform necessary bookkeeping in adding up total purchases, deducting payments, and mailing bills; stock envelopes and bill forms, pay postage, send reminders on unpaid bills, maintain current address information, and try to collect on bad debts.

However, providing the acceptance of bank cards to customers does not come without a significant cost. Banks or other financial institutions that provide credit cards charge the Dealer (merchant in this case) a fee to have the privilege of accepting credit cards. Although fees vary, they generally range from a low of 1.5% to as much as 3% of the total transaction.

Other Forms of Payment

New forms of credit-type payment options are evolving. One of these is the debit card. While they appear similar to an ATM card or major credit card, debit cards allow a consumer to pay for a purchase directly from their checking accounts. This type of card works very similar to a credit card, only the cost of the purchase is debited to the consumers account at the end of the business day. Another type of debit card being tested includes one that is simply a credit card that has an existing credit balance (paid in advance), which is then reduced by the charge made. When the card is slid through a swipe machine, and the transaction amount is transmitted to the appropriate bank, the card is debited for the amount of the transaction. Once the pre-paid balance is used, the card is no longer valid.

Frequency (co-branded) credit cards offer the consumer a specific benefit for continued use of a particular credit card. Frequency bank cards are those that offer some type of incentive for using the card. The best example would be the GM and Ford credit cards. They offer consumers 5% of the transaction value, every time the card is used. The 5% goes into a special rebate account that can be redeemed towards the purchase or lease of a new car or truck. Some Dealers have developed and implemented their own frequency-type programs. **Extreme caution** should be taken with these types of offerings. Contingent liability (the amount of money that would need to be set aside to cover claims by consumers of rebate accounts) can build into substantial amounts. An expert in the field of credit card and/or frequency marketing should be consulted.

Check Cashing

While commonly accounted for as cash, accepting personal or business checks is quite similar to extending credit. It is also a very common way for consumers to pay for products or services. If the check is returned due to in sufficient funds, the dealership has a collection problem on it's hands. Policies and procedures must be developed to provide as much of a safeguard as possible.

There are several companies that offer check protection services to retail establishments. Obviously, these services are provided with some costs. However, it would be wise to assess the potential value of these services, particularly if the dealership receives a significant number of returned checks.

This review of credit and collection procedures has included the value of credit to the dealership; establishment of the dealership's credit policy; responsibility for extending credit; selection of good credit risks, establishment of credit limits and credit controls; collection procedures, including follow-up for past due accounts; and merchant credit card offerings.

INTERNAL CONTROLS OTHER THAN EXPENSES

Little Leaks Sink Big Ships

Internal controls are not necessarily instituted to keep all employees honest and careful. Rather, it is a method by which dishonesty and carelessness is kept to a bare minimum by the establishment of set systems and procedures designed for efficiency in a business-like manner.

Accounts Receivables

One person should be in charge of extending credit and collections. Statements should be mailed promptly at the end of the month.

The subsidiary ledger should be reconciled monthly with the general ledger control account. Accounts receivables schedules should be aged monthly by account with systematic collection follow-up.

Employee accounts, if established, should be shown separately. If employees are provided charge privileges, very strict policies should be implemented, communicated and followed. Bad debt write-off should be the responsibility of the Dealer or a person designated by him.

Finance reserve income receivables should be controlled by making a list of the amounts due on each sale. The amounts collected from the finance company should be compared with such listings to ensure that all revenues from this source have been collected.

Factory Receivables

These should be reconciled by the business manager on a weekly basis, and reviewed by the Dealer. *This account is much too significant not to receive careful attention.* Although they may be titled somewhat different from manufacturer to manufacturer, this receivable account is usually divided into two main areas: warranty claims receivables and new vehicle incentive receivables. Both can amount to large sums of money, particularly with new vehicle incentives.

Accountable Document Control

Accountable documents are the various forms used by the dealership that are accounted for by a numbering system. They include repair orders, parts counter slips, purchase orders, checks, drafts and receipts. Accountable documents should be issued in blocks only to the department managers. These people should be held responsible for safeguarding the numerical sequence of each document until it has been transmitted to the next function.

Only a sufficient quantity (one week supply) should be issued. At the time of issuance, the contents of the package should be checked with the person who signs for them. Any missing documents should be noted immediately.

All unused documents should be kept under lock so that they are accessible only to the assigned person. All users of accountable documents should be cautioned to treat such documents as currency and to safeguard them accordingly when they are absent from their work stations.

The department manager should initial for approval all "no charge" documents. The document should be permanently filed in the dealership records after they have been recorded in the books of original entry. Each document should be numerically accounted for in the accounting department after it is recorded in the books.

Bank Deposits

Vary bank routes at least once each month. If the dealership takes in extremely large amounts of cash, a security company should be considered. Deposits should be made daily.

Bank Reconciliation's

Must be completed by the business manager every month. The Dealer should complete the reconciliation at least once each quarter, or review the reconciliation monthly if it is completed by the computer.

Cash Receipts

All cash receipts should be recorded on serially numbered forms. Cash received during the evening hours or on weekends should be recorded by the manager in charge of a night receipt book. This book should not be in the same numerical sequence being used by the accounting office. Deposits should be made intact and on a daily basis. Receipt books and cash drawers should not be accessible to non-authorized personnel. The person making up bank deposits should not have access to the cash journal, cash receipt journal, or ledger.

Check Writing

All checks should require two signatures. All voided checks should be kept and filed with other recorded checks in numerical order. Before counter signing a check, all supporting documents should be reviewed. Do not pre-sign checks or allow company checks to be made payable to cash.

General

- Duplicate copies of all repair orders and counter slips should be kept in numerical order and accounted for every 30 days.
- Safes and vaults should be used for the keeping of cash, notes, and other assets. Access to these areas of safekeeping should be limited to one person or the smallest number of responsible employees as possible. Combinations or locks should be changed whenever a person with such access leaves the dealership or is assigned to other duties.
- Only one person should be responsible for a specific cash fund.
- Employees in a position of trust should be required to take annual vacations, with relief employees required to report any irregularities they might encounter.
- Pre-numbered memoranda such as checks, sales slips, petty cash vouchers, receipt forms, purchase orders, credit slips and similar items should always be used. A log should be kept listing the names of the persons to whom pre-numbered documents are issued, and a record maintained of the numerical usage.
- Periodic auditing by an independent accounting firm should be standard operating procedure. The firm selected should have previous experience with automobile dealership operations. All employees should be covered by a fidelity bond.

- Alcohol and drugs in the workplace should never be underestimated. Employees heavily involved with either present significant liability potential, health problems, absenteeism, productivity losses and quite often theft problems. An employee hooked on drugs needs cash, and the dealership can become a source for that cash. The dealership should have firm policies regarding drugs and alcohol. Additionally, all managers should be required to attend classes on how to deal with drugs and alcohol in the workplace.

The foregoing suggestions represent a basis for establishing internal controls in a dealership which will prevent most, if not all, losses generally suffered by dealerships through dishonesty, laxity or carelessness.

Inventories

Physical inventory of new and used vehicles should be taken periodically by a person other than sales personnel. Vehicle stock cards with all costs and liability data recorded on them should be maintained. A physical inventory of parts and accessories should be taken at least once a year by an outside agency, and reconciled with the perpetual inventory. Inventories of all items, other than parts and accessories, should be taken monthly.

Only items covered by repair orders, counter slips or requisitions should be issued from inventory. It should be ascertained that all inventories are covered by insurance against fire and theft.

The parts department and store room areas containing inventories should be kept locked when not in use, and access to these areas should be carefully controlled.

Incoming Mail

The Dealer should open and date-stamp all mail. If this is not practical, then the Dealer should appoint a responsible person for this duty, and request a list of all incoming checks for a future audit.

Office Supplies

Should be stored in a locked cabinet or storage room. One person should be responsible for the inventory and distribution of the supplies.

Parts Counter Slips

Must be in numerical sequence. Missing slips must be accounted for, and all counter slips should be filled out in ink.

Parts Control

No one should have access to the parts department, except authorized personnel. The department should be locked at night. Parts should be stored in their appropriate bins immediately on receipt. Invoices should be checked against shipments when they are received.

Payroll

It should be confirmed that only employees are on the payroll. When a person is removed from the payroll, fringe benefits should be checked to make sure they are not continuing to be paid. A time limit should be set for holding unclaimed wages, and they should be kept by the Dealer rather than by a bookkeeper or payroll clerk.

All wages or salary increases should be handled on a written form and have the Dealer's approval indicated. A separate impress bank account should be used for payrolls.

Hard copies of repair orders should be cross-checked against technicians' time tickets. This should be done by the accounting department, and it should be checked periodically against the time reports prepared by the shop foreman or service manager.

Petty Cash

Vouchers should be numbered and approved by department managers in ink.

Purchases

All purchases should require the issuance of a pre-numbered purchase order. The second copy should agree with vendor invoice when received, and be signed by authorized personnel only. Distribution of purchase order books should be limited to one or two managers.

Repair Order Log

Account for each repair order by number. Voided repair orders must be noted for accountability and signed by department manager.

Special Tools

Tools should be locked in secured area. They should be issued and checked for return by one individual. A periodic (monthly) inventory should be performed.

Sublet Repairs

A log should be maintained and all sublet repair invoices should be checked.

Supplies and Materials

Review usage of rags, cleaners, solvents, uniforms, and paint on recurring basis. There should also be a slight charge for these types of supplies on customer-pay repair orders, where appropriate.

Used Car Values

Weekly or bi-monthly top management reviews of trades taken in to verify current market values and reconditioning plans. Monthly review should also include sales of wholesaled vehicles.

Paper Flow - Sales

Precise policies concerning proper completion of all new and used vehicle sales paperwork and the receipt of any cash due from deposits or due at delivery. Audit procedures must also be implemented that include a "double-check" system for sales commissions. The Dealer or general manager should make surprise audits of sales paperwork (deal jackets) at least every other month.

Warranty Log

Warranty receivables schedules by repair order number must be checked against payments received and ledger balances.

Regulatory Compliance

All businesses, including Dealerships are faced with numerous governmentally-mandated regulations. These regulations may come from federal, state or local governing bodies. Some of these regulatory requirements include:

- FTC Used Car Buyers Guide
- New Vehicle Monroney Labeling
- IRS Cash Reporting Rule
- Hiring/Firing Discrimination
- Hazardous Chemical Labeling, Training and Communications
- Express and Implied Warranties
- Truth in Lending
- OSHA (Occupational Safety and Health Administration) Safety Regulations
- EPA Underground Gasoline/Oil Tank Storage
- EPA Hazardous Chemical Waste Disposal

These are just a few of the many important regulations that effect the dealership operation. Every Dealer and manager must be aware of those that affect the various departments of the dealership. Failure to comply can result in fines costing tens of thousands of dollars. In more severe cases, such as non-compliance with EPA regulations, those costs can go well into the hundreds of thousands. Quarterly reviews of legal compliance should be made by the Dealer. If necessary, the services of a professional risk manager should be sought.

Summary

This chapter reviewed the importance of a sound credit management system. This system included the establishment of policies and procedures, along with the designation of a person responsible for carry them out. Because accounts receivables can put a drain on the dealership's cash flow position, emphasis was put on the practice of these procedures as well as consistent follow-up and collection procedures.

Also reviewed was internal controls exclusive of operating expense accounts. These included receivable accounts, accountable document control, bank-related functions, inventories and supplies, general topics, regulatory issues, paper flow and warranty.

CHAPTER V

WHOLESALE FINANCING

Background

Financing or the obtaining of funds (capital) for use in a business is often called Wholesale Financing. All businesses require money for: operating expenses, operating equipment, furniture and fixtures, signs, supplies and inventories. The most common wholesale financing is a Capital Loan, where the business borrows a large sum of money to be used for one or more of the above reasons. This capital loan is paid back over a long period of time, usually five years, at a stated interest rate. For example, a $500,000 capital loan over a five year pay back might be paid off as follows: $100,000 principal pay back each year plus the interest on the unpaid balance. At a 10% simple interest charge the first year pay off would be $100,000 principle plus $50,000 in interest ($500,000 X 10%) for a total of $150,000. In one sense, a mortgage is a type of financing where the principle and interest are paid off over an extended period of time, generally 20 -30 years. However, mortgages are not considered as wholesale financing.

In the automobile business, vehicle inventories represent a vast amount of capital, because of their high per unit cost. Very few Dealers, usually small, well-capitalized ones, can afford to pay for their own inventories. With the average cost of a new vehicle being $16,000 - $18,000, an inventory of 100 units would require $1,600,000 - $1,800,000, an amount too large for most any Dealer. In order to have operating capital available to pay operating expenses, purchase parts, equipment, supplies, etc., it became a necessity to finance Vehicle Inventory through other means. This financing is called New Car Floor Planning, and is made available through factory and distributor finance companies, banks, and other financial institutions.

New Car Floor Planning

When a finance institution is requested to establish a wholesale floor plan credit line for a dealership, the finance company meets with the Dealer principal to determine the total amount of credit necessary to satisfy normal inventory requirements. This is commonly referred to as the credit line. Although peak selling periods are conceded to require higher-than-average inventories and credit limits, normal inventory requirements are used as a guide in setting the credit line. When this credit line is being established, the first factor considered is the Dealer's rate of travel.

The term, "rate of travel," is a term used to indicate the number of new cars and trucks that the Dealer sells, on an average, each month. For example, a Dealer with a 600-car potential can be expected to sell 600 cars per year, or 50 cars per month. Therefore, 50 cars per month is said to be the dealership's rate of travel. If the dealership also sells 600 trucks per year, the rate of travel on trucks is also 50 per month, bringing the total rate of travel to 100 new units per month.

It would be difficult to establish a hard and fast rule as to how many days' supply of new units a Dealer should carry in his inventory. However, on average, days supply should be kept at around 45-60 days. A Dealer in a farming area, where buying habits are geared to the marketing of crops, may need a large inventory during the harvest and marketing season, but a smaller inventory at other times. A large metropolitan Dealer may have as many as twenty cars on the showroom floor at all times, while a small Dealer in a country town may have one or two. Seasonal selling conditions must also be considered. Northern dealerships may need 60 to 90 days during peak spring selling seasons, while winter months may require around 30-45 days.

An example of how a line of credit is established for a dealership follows:

A dealership has sold 3,600 cars over the past three years for an average of 1,200 per year. The "rate of travel" is 100 (1,200 divided by 12). The finance company and Dealer agree on a 45-day supply of vehicles that will be inventoried on an average.

$$100 = 30 \text{ days' supply}$$
$$\underline{50} = \underline{15} \text{ days' supply}$$
$$150 = 45 \text{ days' supply}$$

Using an average cost of vehicle of $16,000, then $16,000 x 150 = $2,400,000. The finance company then informs the factory or distributor that the Credit Line is $2,400,000. Beyond this total amount of dollars, the finance company will not pay for additional units.

The factory then drafts the finance company on each car shipped to the dealership.

Approval and Delivery

Once the wholesale floor plan credit line has been established the Dealer must instruct the factory to draft on the finance institution establishing the credit line to obtain payment for new cars and trucks shipped. The finance institution notifies the factory that the Dealer is approved for wholesale credit.

Notification of the factory by the finance institution includes the type of approval granted. The four most common types of wholesale floor planning approval are blanket approval, advance notice of shipment, signature plan and direct wholesale method.   In a very few cases Dealers are allowed to operate on a C.O.D. basis. The manufacturers are very reluctant to agree to this, because they have no guarantee of payment at the time the order is placed.

Blanket approval, as the name implies, enables the factory to collect automatically for all new cars and trucks shipped to a Dealer. The factory merely drafts the finance institution by invoice, knowing in advance that all shipments will be approved. Payment is then made, usually by electronic funds transfer (EFT).

Advance notice of shipment requires the factory to notify the finance institution of all contemplated shipments to the Dealer. It may be done either by the factory informing the finance institution directly, or by notifying the Dealer, who relays the notification to the finance institution. In either case, the finance institution has the opportunity to refuse payment by so informing the factory prior to shipment.

Signature plans basically involve vehicles purchased at factory sponsored auctions. Any financing instruments and other documents are prepared by the participating auction and executed by the Dealer or the Dealer's authorized agent. The finance institution arranges to make payment (usually electronic) to the auction.

The Direct Wholesale method involves Dealer inventory acquired through the purchase from or exchange with other Dealers. All documents are prepared by the Dealer and it is the responsibility of the Dealer to release any existing security interest, obtain negotiable title or Manufacturers Statement of Origin.

Under the blanket approval and advance notice of shipping plans, new units are shipped directly to the Dealer by the factory. To assist Dealers from paying interest on floor plan units prior to arrival at the dealership, factories provide a free floor plan interest period. Under one method, the factory refunds to the Dealer a percentage of each invoice amount.

Documentation

In most states, the law governing wholesale financing is covered by either the Uniform Commercial Code or the Uniform Trust Receipts Law. Under the Uniform Commercial Code, the following forms are used: (a) agreement for wholesale financing, and (b) secretary's certificate of resolution for wholesale financing (for corporations only).

The agreement for wholesale financing is the underlying agreement between the Dealer and the finance institution. It outlines the conditions under which funds will be advanced for the Dealer to cover vehicles shipped by the factory or purchased from other Dealers or distributors. The following basic points are covered in the agreement.

- The finance institution will pay the factory or distributor for units obtained for a Dealer's inventory as requested by the Dealer
- The Dealer will sign the wholesale billing sent to him by the finance institution to acknowledge his debt; the debt will also be considered acknowledged if the Dealer does not notify the finance institution by registered mail, within five days of the date that the wholesale billing was mailed to him, of any corrections or objections to the billing
- The Dealer agrees to pay the finance institution immediately upon sale of the financed unit. He or she further agrees to pay interest and other charges at the current rate
- The chattels (vehicles) will be insured by the Dealer for their full value against outlined risks, typically theft, vandalism and collision
- The finance institution has the right to examine the chattels from time to time, and the books (inventory record) relating to these chattels
- The finance institution will control the amount of credit extended at all times
- The Dealer will not use the floor planned units, unless placed into demonstrator service

The reader is reminded that all approvals for floor planning are contingent on the Dealer being within the pre-established credit line limit.

The secretary's certificate of resolution for wholesale financing is essentially a limited power of attorney. It is used only when the dealership is a corporation (as most are), and it gives the president, vice-president or treasurer of the corporation the authority to enter into an agreement for wholesale financing with a finance institution.

Under the Uniform Trust Receipts Law, the following forms are used: (a) Dealer application for floor plan credit; (b) consent to sign; (c) resolution of board of directors (for corporations only); (d) trust receipt; and (e) statement of trust receipt financing.

The Dealer application for floor plan credit (like the agreement under the Commercial Code) is the underlying agreement between the Dealer and the finance institution. Following are the basic points covered in the Dealer application for floor plan credit.

- The credit line is established and controlled by the finance institution
- The Dealer will execute trust receipts, or other designated documents, in favor of the finance institution for the amount of credit extended
- The Dealer admits and guarantees the finance institution's security interest in the merchandise delivered to him and agrees to hold it in trust for the said institution
- The Dealer agrees not to use the merchandise, and to pay for it promptly when sold
- The Dealer acknowledges that the finance institution may examine the merchandise and the books related to it at any time
- The Dealer agrees to pay interest at the current rate and other charges for the credit extended, including charges for insurance if it is not provided by the Dealer directly

The consent-to-sign document is a limited power of attorney, giving the finance institution the authority to prepare the lien documents and to sign them for the Dealer. This eliminates the need for obtaining a signed document before funds are advanced to the manufacturer on behalf of the Dealer. It saves considerable time and inconvenience for the Dealer, the manufacturer and the finance institution.

The resolution of the board of directors, used only with corporations, is a statement attesting to the fact that a meeting of the board of directors was held and that the board agreed to permit an officer of the corporation to give power of attorney (consent to sign) to the finance institution for the purpose of signing wholesale floor plan lien documents.

The trust receipt is the lien document, or security instrument, which acknowledges the debt of the Dealer to the finance institution for the wholesale credit that has been extended.

The statement of trust receipt financing is signed by the finance institution and the Dealer. It is filed by the finance institution with a public officer, usually the clerk of the court or Secretary of State. It gives notice that the finance institution has entrusted merchandise to the Dealer. The statement of trust receipt financing is good for a period of twelve months after filing, eliminating the need for filing each individual trust receipt covering each shipment of merchandise. At the end of twelve months, the finance institution may extend the document's validity for an additional twelve months by filing an affidavit of renewal which need not be signed by the Dealer. After the second year, a new statement of trust receipt financing must be signed and filed.

Inventory Check

As has been noted, extension of floor plan credit to a Dealer involves a substantial amount of money. The finance institution's investment in the Dealer's inventory often runs in seven figures, and can exceed several million dollars for larger Dealer accounts.

The finance institution is quite willing to make this credit available to financially sound Dealers who create a substantial volume of retail finance paper. It is the retail paper which creates the profit in the finance business. However, the finance institution will not extend credit, even to a financially sound Dealer, if he or she does not honor the wholesale financing agreement by paying for floor planned cars promptly when they are sold, and by keeping the unsold units in his inventory unused at all times.

To safeguard its investment, and help sustain its agreement with the Dealer, the finance institution makes a periodic (usually monthly) physical check of the Dealer's inventory. This check is a standard procedure in the finance industry. It is in no way a reflection about the Dealer's integrity.

Interest and Flat Charge

The cost of new car floor planning consists of two factors, interest and flat charge. The interest rate varies with the prime rate. It is usually between 1/2% to 1% above the current prime rate. However, some Dealers have been able to negotiate slightly lower rates. In some cases, finance institutions will provide some floor plan rate reductions if a certain level of retail finance penetration is received. Thus, if the prime rate is 10%, the interest rate for new car floor planning would be 11%. The prime rate is considered the standard interest rate charged by lending institutions to their best (capital base and credit reputation) corporate clients.

Finance companies charge Dealers by the month for floor plan interest. Interest is calculated based on the daily outstanding balance. For example: if the current rate is 11%, the daily charge would be 11% or .000301 (.11 divided by 365 days). If on May 1, the Dealership's outstanding balance was $1,800,000, that day's charge would be $541.80. Putting that into perspective, the monthly floor plan cost would then be in the area of $16,000. Obviously, daily balances change, influencing the actual total monthly floor plan charge.

The second factor involved in the cost of inventory flooring is the flat rate charge. This flat rate charge is made to cover a portion of the cost of maintaining special facilities for the payment of invoices at assembly and shipping points, for the appraisal, examining and verifying of Dealer inventories, and, where insurance is provided, to cover its cost. There are, therefore, two different flat charges. One is a with-insurance flat charge; the other is without insurance.

Although the with-insurance flat charge varies somewhat, the typical charge is one - eighth of one percent of a unit's invoice cost for each ninety days, or fraction thereof, remaining in inventory. Thus, on a $16,000 car, the charge would be $20.00 for ninety days. Insurance coverage includes fire, theft, malicious mischief or vandalism, external discharge or leakage of water, falling aircraft, riot or civil commotion, transportation (damage caused by stranding, sinking, burning, collision, or derailment of any conveyance on which an automobile is transported on land or over water, except that vehicles conveyed in or upon any motor vehicle, semi-trailer or trailer are protected only for a specified amount), and acts of God (cyclone, earthquake, flood or rising water, hail, lightning, tornado and windstorm). Coverage is from the date of purchase or transport to the date of payment or sale at retail, while enroute to and at the Dealer's place of business or storage, body plant or paint shop, and while the unit is displayed in an automobile show, exhibitions, fairs and bazaars in the United States or Canada.

Since some manufacturers do not draft the finance company for payment until the estimated date of arrival at the dealership, such manufacturers assume all risk of damage (except those borne by the carrier) while the vehicles are in transit to the Dealer. Accordingly, the insurance coverage previously itemized would start from the date on which the Dealer takes possession of the units.

When insurance is not provided by the finance institution, the Dealer must furnish the finance institution with a copy of the policy covering the inventory, and it must be named as payee in the event of loss. The flat charge usually is 1/12 of 1% of the invoice cost for ninety days. Taking the same $16,000 car, used previously as an example, the flat charge would be $13.28 or $6.72 less than with-insurance flat charge.

An additional form of insurance available to Dealers who handle their wholesale floor planning on a with-insurance basis through the finance institution is the drive-away coverage. This type of insurance covers any collision damage which might be sustained while the vehicle is being driven from the factory to the Dealer's place of business.

Although rare, from time to time, the Dealer finds it necessary to send an employee to the factory to pick up and drive back a new car which has been ordered for a customer. Since the car would be exposed to collision damage during the trip to the dealership, but will not be driven after it arrives, collision coverage is needed for this period of time only. Cost of this coverage varies with the cost of the car itself and the distance it is to be driven. There is no need for such coverage when the car is shipped to the Dealer by truck or rail transportation.

Used Car Floor Planning

Used car floor planning must be avoided. Under normal circumstances, the Dealer should have sufficient capital to carry the used car inventory. Dealers who find it necessary to employ used car floor planning on a permanent basis are very likely under-capitalized or their used car merchandising operation is poorly managed. The principle purpose of used car flooring is to assist Dealers temporarily during periods when new car sales are so active that trade-ins are being acquired more rapidly than they can be reconditioned and sold. Even in that type of situation, the Dealer should be able to wholesale units quickly to raise needed capital. Used car floor planning is expensive - usually 1% to 11/2% above new car interest rates.

One major exception to used car floor planning is the purchase of manufacturer vehicles at the auction. These vehicles are typically those used by the manufacturers employees, rental vehicles or other special use vehicles. These vehicles are generally less than one year old, have only a few thousand miles on them, and are sold (auctioned) at special factory sales. Because the purchase costs can be high, it is very common to floor plan these units, particularly if the Dealer is buying a large number of factory vehicles. In most cases, these units are added to the new vehicle floor plan account.

There is really only one other situation that might justify floor planning used cars. If the dealership has taken in an usually high number of trades that could be retailed, rather than wholesaled, floor planning provides the temporary relief. In that situation, the Dealer will be able to sell the used cars at retail, rather than wholesaling them immediately at no profit, or even at some loss. However, floor planning used cars **should not** become standard operating procedure.

Several factors must be considered when a used car wholesale line is established. Included are the cash needs of the Dealer, the size of the used car operation, and the Dealer's net worth. Since used car flooring is normally a temporary accommodation, and is not intended to cover the entire used car inventory, the amount of credit extended is usually well within the limit that good business dictates in view of the Dealer's net worth.

Lien documents for used car wholesale financing vary from state to state, depending on the legislation in effect. In some cases the trust receipt is used, as with new car flooring, and the same statement of trust receipt financing is filed. The same is also true in certain states with respect to the Uniform Commercial Code. In still other states, a signed chattel mortgage must be obtained and filled for each used car or group of used cars floored.

When a Dealer finds it necessary to floor plan used cars, the usual procedure is to notify the finance institution of the amount of cash needed and to furnish a list of automobiles which will be used as collateral. Normally, only private passenger cars of the current or four previous model years qualify for used car flooring. These cars, of course, must be in salable condition, and they must represent makes and models which can be readily resold in the local market. Quite often, the finance institution will inspect the collateral before any funds are advanced.

The amount of money advanced on each car is normally limited to a percentage of the average loan value of the unit as set forth in an approved used car guide book. The usual percentage is approximately 80% of the loan value of the car. This not only provides the necessary security desired by the finance institution, but also affords the Dealer some cash when the unit is sold and the lien is paid.

Vehicles floor planned by a Dealer must, of course, be owned by the dealership free and clear of any liens. Evidence of ownership, such as the certificate of title or a bill of sale showing the title is being applied for, must be furnished.

Used cars which have been floor planned are checked periodically by the finance institution, the same as the new car flooring. Since the extension of credit is based on a particular car, the amount floor planned must be paid in full when the car is sold.

It was noted earlier that the cost of new car floor planning is based on two factors, interest and flat charge. The same is true of used car flooring costs. The interest rate, as stated earlier, is normally 1% to 1.5% higher than new car rates. A charge is made for the actual number of days the money is in use and is computed by the average daily balance method, just as in the case of new car flooring.

Flat charges vary in different localities, approximating $2.00 to $3.00 per unit for each ninety days. Insurance is rarely included in used car floor planning. Therefore, the Dealer must furnish his or her own coverage. This coverage should be the same as that for new cars. It is often handled under a blanket coverage policy which includes all used cars in inventory, as well as new vehicles owned outright by the Dealer.

Used cars are usually floored for an initial period of thirty days. This period may be extended for additional thirty-day periods. However, in that event, balances are usually curtailed each month since loan values of used cars decline from month to month. Curtailment is simply a flat payment to reduce principal, and is usually 2.5% of the floor plan amount.

It can't be stated too many times: Used car floor planning should be avoided.

Demonstrator Financing

For many years, one of the basic factors of selling automobiles has been the demonstration drive. The prospective buyer of an automobile expects the dealership to provide an opportunity to drive the kind of car he or she plans to buy. For the salesperson, the demonstration drive is one of the most effective methods used to influence the prospect's decision.

To benefit from the advantages of a demonstration drive, Dealers made demonstrators available for the use of salespeople and managers. Today, Dealers vary greatly on policies regarding demonstrators. Some have eliminated them all together, while others provide them only to management. Still, in other cases, Dealer provide them and charge the user for the privilege. In those situations, the charge varies as well, with some providing demonstrators free of charge based on performance.

If demonstrators are provided, and to avoid depletion of operating capital, the Dealer must finance those units placed into service. This is typically done through the finance institution that provides the Dealer's new vehicle floor plan. In this case, it is necessary to establish a demonstrator credit line, just the same as new car and used car floor plan credit lines must be established. For this purpose, consideration must be given to the size of the Dealer sales organization, the Dealer's net worth, and the Dealer's method of operation. Obviously, the Dealer who employs 30 salespeople and managers needs considerably more demonstrators than the Dealer who employs only five.

The Dealer's net worth is also considered when establishing a demonstrator line, just as it is in any extension of credit to the Dealer.

Documentation

There are two basic documents used in financing demonstrators. In the case of the house demonstrator, the original trust receipt used when the car was floor planned carries over. If the car was purchased from the factory or the distributor and paid for by the finance institution, then set up originally as a house demonstrator without being floor planned, a trust receipt is also used. If the car to be set up as a house demonstrator is owned by the Dealer and is not open on the wholesale floor plan, the lien document to be used will be a trust receipt in some states, and a chattel mortgage in others. The local state laws would govern the document used.

Operation of the Plan

When the Dealer wishes to place a unit in service as a demonstrator, the finance institution is advised. As noted earlier, no separate lien document is needed if the unit is currently being floor planned. The finance institution merely rebills the unit as a demonstrator and sends a copy of the billing to the Dealer. Once each month, the Dealer is billed for the interest charges on the average daily balance method and for the monthly principle payment.

State laws vary on the licensing and registration of demonstrators. In some states the vehicle does not have to be licensed or titled, and may be driven with a Dealer License Plate. In other states, the demonstrator must be titled and licensed the same way as that for a retail sale to a consumer.

The interest rates for a house demonstrator are usually the same as the rates for new car wholesale, plus insurance (including collision) and nominal flat charges. The demonstrator must be curtailed monthly with minimum payments of 2.0% to 2.5% of the amount financed. The maturity of the contract might be six months with five monthly payments and a balloon payment on the sixth month, or it may go right back into inventory, once taken out of demonstrator service. This period of time is often preferred because it keeps the demonstrator from becoming a "used" car with high mileage and shopworn appearance.

For those dealerships that do not provide demonstrators, salespeople and managers are usually provided special purchase pricing by the manufacturer, and special financing or leasing is also provided.

Interest rates for the salesperson-owned demonstrator plan are normally set substantially lower than those rates made available to the retail customer. These rates will vary in different areas. Physical damage insurance covering the automobile and credit life insurance covering the unpaid balance are also available and may be financed with the car.

Summary

This chapter reviewed the different types of wholesale financing, and their importance. Floor planning of new vehicles is a critical element in the daily operation of a dealership. It is also an expensive part of the business should be carefully monitored. Monitoring should include both inventory turn (days supply) and security of the new vehicles on hand.

CHAPTER 6

CHAPTER VI

RETAIL FINANCING

Overview

When this country was first settled, an individual's work was principally directed toward basic survival needs. People produced their own food and clothing, and obtained their own fuel for cooking and heating their homes. The family unit was largely self-sufficient and bartered for necessities which it did not or could not self-produce. However, movement away from an agrarian economy towards an industrial one saw many people leave their farms, moving to the cities to work in factories, in transportation, and in commerce. The relative security of self-sufficiency was abandoned for a money wage, which was then exchanged for the goods someone else produced.

Continued improvements in technology and market expansion led to the development of factories capable of producing immense quantities of goods. Correspondingly, economies of scale possible with mass production led to lower prices and better value. Yet, if markets were to be restricted only to customers who would pay cash, the demand for many goods would be significantly restricted, and extensive mass production would be restricted as well. To pass on to the consumer the optimum economies of scale realized through mass production, some financial mechanisms became essential which would make it possible to buy goods as they were produced and to pay for them as they were being used.

The financial mechanism developed to meet that need was installment credit. The extension of that credit is based upon the premise that a wage earner with a steady income and good character can be trusted to repay an obligation. Such credit gives the consumer immediate use of the goods or services in exchange for a promise to pay a specific sum in a definite number of periodic future payments. Installment credit opens up the full market for goods and services by making customers of people lacking ready cash for goods and services needed or desired. And, while the expense of consumer credit becomes another cost added to the finished product or service provided, that cost becomes insignificant when compared with the lower prices made possible by mass production and mass service. Thus, all consumers benefit in lower prices, even those cash buyers who pride themselves on never using credit. Because credit is readily available, consumers enjoy a higher standard of living then they would otherwise, and total output of goods and services is greater. The promise to pay may be an information understanding to pay an open account, or it may be a formal agreement spelled out in a negotiable instrument which contains provisions for legal action in case of default.

Credit needs of the consumer are met in numerous ways. Some institutions limit themselves to selling goods or services on time payments, while others will lend cash to be used in paying accumulated bills or in making new purchases. Some provide credit cards which will be honored for purchases at many retail establishments. These institutions may deal with the credit consumer face to face or through a third party.

Sales Finance Companies

In 1910, some half a million American families owned an automobile, a luxury purchased for cash. Primarily, the well-to-do who could afford the lump sum purchase possessed those early automobiles.

However, it was soon obvious that demand for the economic and social benefits brought about through ownership of personal transportation created a potentially unlimited automobile market. If some means could be instituted for financing the purchase of those coveted automobiles, that market could be tapped. Not only were most individuals unable to raise the cash necessary to purchase a single automobile, early automobile Dealers and factories also operated with limited capital. Market development was curtailed by the inadequacy of financial resources.

To correct this deficiency, a new kind of finance institution needed to be organized to provide loans to the Dealers to finance their inventories and to make arrangements whereby their retail customers could make time payments for their purchases. Alfred P. Sloan had that vision. If General Motors could provide the necessary financing, both to Dealers and consumers, they would benefit through the sale of more automobiles. Therefore, in 1919 he helped to found the General Motors Acceptance Corporation (GMAC). Although Sloan's competitor, Henry Ford was reluctant at first, his company eventually followed with the establishment of Ford Motor Credit Company after World War II.

These institutions, originally called finance companies, have matured and are often organized today along functional lines, i.e., sales financing to aid in the purchase of consumer goods and commercial financing to assist in the acquisition of capital goods.

As installment financing proved its value in the financing of new cars, it was extended to used cars and finally to other consumer goods. Special regulatory laws were passed in several states: motor vehicle finance laws, installment finance laws, usury laws, and "other goods" installment sales laws.

As installment financing, in it's traditional sense, evolved, so to did the price of new and used cars and trucks. This created a need for lending institutions to become more "creative" with the terms and conditions of installment financing. Thus, alternative financing methods such as leasing became available. Other alternative methods included balloon notes which consisted of lower payments during the term of the loan, with one larger payment at the end of the loan. Today, leasing has become one of the most popular alternatives to installment financing.

Today's automotive-related consumer installment credit volume is immense. As reported by NADA's Automotive Executive magazine, (August, 1995) automotive installment credit outstanding in 1994 accounted for 35.7% of all consumer credit, amounting to 325 billion dollars. To accommodate this volume, several thousand sales finance companies operate throughout the United States. A few are giant institutions with complete national coverage. There are also many good-sized regional companies, and many more are small operations with one or more branches.

Direct Financing

Direct financing is limited to a two-party transaction where the consumer borrows directly from the original lender. From there, the consumer makes their purchase. An example would be a new vehicle customer borrowing the money for the purchase directly from a bank, credit union, savings and loan association, or even a friend or relative.

Indirect Financing

Indirect financing adds one or more parties to the direct financing relationship. These are identified as Financial Intermediaries. They are part of the commercial banking system as your local bank, credit union or savings and loan association. Outside of that system, institutions such as Ford Motor Credit, GMAC

Chrysler Finance and others handle indirect financing. In either case, these intermediaries create loans by using reserves developed through debt or equity financing. An example of debt would be the purchase of bank bonds. An example of equity would be the purchase of bank stock.

In today's world, almost all financing is "indirect" due to the realization that a borrower, if he or she dealt with enough individuals, did not have to keep on hand an amount equal to what he had borrowed. This is a very simplified discussion of why a bank can lend out more money than it has on deposit and make profits. This is not practical for an individual.

Financing Control

Control in consumer financing involves the last Financial Intermediary to relate to the ultimate consumer. If an automobile purchaser borrows from the bank, the bank has control. Likewise, if that consumer signs a bank contract at a dealership, the Dealer has control. Control is important because a commission is paid to the last Financial Intermediary. In the Dealer's case, it may make an unacceptable cash transaction an acceptable finance contract.

Dealer Credit Business

Dealer business is a credit institution's method of acquiring consumer installment credit obligations from the seller of the merchandise. In these transactions, the seller, such as a automobile Dealer, takes the credit application and prepares the note and conditional sales contract, lease or other security agreement. The Dealer contacts the financial institution to ask whether, on the basis of the information submitted, it will accept the purchaser as a customer and buy the paper (approve the lease or loan).

Three primary parties are involved in the transaction: The purchaser, the Dealer, and the finance institution. The finance institution buys the retail paper from the Dealer usually for the face amount of the note, less the finance charge. The purchaser is notified at the closing of the sale of his or her obligation to the lender. The customer is also is instructed to make payment directly to the finance institution, which may never see the consumer unless collection problems arise.

Advantages of Dealer business are realized by both the Dealer and the finance institution. Roughly 80% of new cars and 75% of used cars are bought on credit or are leased. Financing and leasing helps the Dealer significantly in generating sizable volumes of sales and resulting profit. Dealers bring a greater volume of business to the finance institution than they themselves can generate in their normal course of business, and in a shorter period of time.

To remain competitive with other lenders, finance institutions must understand the Dealers' operation, and they must provide fast and efficient service. In the past, it would take several hours (sometimes one whole day) after an application was submitted to gain approval. With the advantage of today's computer technology, Dealers get notification of credit approval or denial generally within 60 minutes, and sometimes within just a few minutes. Finance institutions must also provide consistent coverage, competitive rates, and effective collection follow-up. They may also need to be capable of financing the Dealer's inventory requirements.

Dealer business does create some risk for finance institutions. Therefore, they must take certain precautions to limit that risk. Dealers should be thoroughly informed about the institution's policies and methods of conducting business. Speed is essential to expedite the sale. However the finance institution does need sufficient time to assure itself of the credit worthiness of the purchaser, particularly in marginal cases. While the paper acquired should be predicated on the analysis of the purchaser's credit standing, some weight is given in marginal cases to the Dealer and the nature of each individual case.

Although it is becoming more rare, finance institutions may evaluate the Dealer's own credit reputation, the quality of goods he offers for sale, the quality of service he provides, and whether he generally conducts his business in satisfactory manner. Consumer dissatisfaction with a Dealer can also produce problems for the finance institution. The purchaser may believe it to be appropriate to take their anger at the Dealer out on the lender directly. This may include the stoppage of monthly payments.

In recent history, dealerships have become sound local businesses, not usually subject to some of the financing dishonesty of the past. There have been Dealers who exposed finance institutions to various types of unethical practices and have even defrauded some on occasion. Some of these practices have included fictitious credit applications, forged contracts, misrepresentation of down payment, misrepresentation of goods sold, and failure to deliver goods sold. Others are misappropriation by Dealers of monthly payments, past-due payments remitted by Dealers to avoid payment in full required on defaulted paper, sale of repossessed goods by the Dealer without payment of the net balance due, and duplicate paper discounted with two or more finance institutions.

To protect themselves against the possibility of fraud, credit institutions have been forced to implement measures and controls, including continuous checkups.

Finance Plans

Numerous plans for the financing of cars and trucks are available through finance companies, banks and manufacturer finance divisions. Although there may be very slight differences, they are not too significant departures from basic concepts. The plan of one finance institution generally resembles its counterpart offered by another institution. There are some state laws that impact what finance plans may be offered, including some that limit the Dealer's financial exposure.

For the purpose of this chapter, examples for the different retail finance plans have been provided courtesy of The Ford Motor Credit Company. Again, while this is specific to Ford Motor Credit, most lending institutions' plans are similar.

Without - Recourse Plan

In most states, finance institutions make arrangements to buy finance contracts from the Dealer on a without-recourse basis. Notwithstanding, the assignment of such contracts on a without-recourse basis, the Dealer remains fully responsible for a pro-rata portion of any refund paid or credited to the retail customer, and to the extent of the rate differential paid or credited to the dealer for any such contracts, for the amount of any net loss sustained by the lending institution in connection with defaulted contracts, as stated in "refunds for Anticipated Contract," found later in this chapter.

Essentially, without-recourse means the Dealer has no financial liability if a customer defaults on the payments to the lender, except for any reserve that might be owed the Dealer from the original sale of the contract. This assumes the dealership complied with all requirements such as full disclosure and representation, accurate completion of finance documents and any other provisions that might be required by the lender at the time of the sale.

Repurchase Plan

The repurchase assignment, generally found on the reverse side of the contract, provides that the Dealer guarantees payment of the full amount remaining unpaid under the contract and agrees to pay such amount to the lending institution if the customer defaults in the payment of any installment, except as otherwise provided by any special terms that may be in effect at that time. Additionally, there are other exceptions, listed under "Exceptions to Limitations on Dealer's Responsibility," detailed later in this chapter. Generally, the Dealer's responsibility under contracts assigned on a repurchase basis will be limited to repurchasing from the lending institution any contract covering a vehicle repossessed by such lending institution and returned to the Dealer as follows:

- If the vehicle is a passenger car or light commercial vehicle (16,000 lbs. GVW or less), it must be returned to the Dealer's place of business not later than 90 days after maturity of the earliest installment still more than 50% in default, unless the Dealer has agreed to a longer redelivery period. If efforts to repossess are impeded by bankruptcy proceedings, litigation (except litigation filed by the lending institution to obtain possession of the vehicle) or legislation of executive proclamation, the redelivery period will be extended for the greater of: (1) 15 days beyond the lending institution's receiving actual notice of the removal of such impediment (in the case of bankruptcy, the impediment shall not be deemed to have been removed until the lending institution has received written notice of the removal of such impediment from the bankruptcy court by mail), or (2) the number of days remaining in the original 90-day or longer redelivery period.

If the vehicle is a medium or heavy commercial vehicle over (16,000 lbs. GVW), it must be returned to the Dealer within 90 days after the maturity of the earliest installment still more than 50% in default, however, the vehicle shall be deemed to have been returned to the Dealer by storing it for the account (and at the expense) of the Dealer in the vicinity of the place of repossession and upon giving notice thereof to the Dealer, unless the Dealer has agreed to a longer redelivery period. If efforts to repossess are impeded by bankruptcy proceedings, litigation (except litigation filed by the lending institution to obtain possession of the vehicle), legislation or executive proclamation, the redelivery period will be extended for the greater of (1) 30 days beyond the lending institution's receiving actual notice of the removal of such impediment (in the case of bankruptcy, the impediment shall not be deemed to have been removed until the lending institution has received written notice of the removal of such impediment from the bankruptcy court by mail), or (2) the number of days remaining in the original 90-day or longer redelivery period.

Repurchase Price

The repurchase price to the Dealer for each contract covering a passenger car or light commercial vehicle repossessed by the lending institution and returned to the Dealer, as provided above, shall be the amount remaining unpaid under the contract, including accumulated late charges, less the following amounts:

- The unearned portion of the lending institution's discount charge with respect to the contract.
- With respect to a vehicle which at the time of repossession is not more than six model years old (including the current series): the replacement value of any of the following items if missing at the time of repossession -- engine, transmission, battery, radio, air conditioner (except portable radios), and tires and wheels. To be eligible, the equipment claimed as missing must have been on the vehicle at the time of delivery and must be described on the factory invoice and/or buyer's order as to size, model, type or other description sufficient to permit determination of replacement value.

- With respect to a vehicle covered by deductible collision insurance and damage prior to repossession by any collision in an amount greater than the deductible: the amount of the deductible applicable to each collision loss, but not in excess of $500 per collision
- With respect to a vehicle that at the time of sale to the customer was eight model years old or less, and on which the original unpaid amount financed was $1,000 or less and was not covered by collision insurance (see Other Dealer Responsibility): the amount of any collision damage resulting from a single direct collision prior to repossession. The amount allowed to the Dealer for loss or damage to such vehicle, as provided above, will be limited to the lesser of; (1) the Dealer's replacement cost of such vehicle, or (2) the amount remaining unpaid under the contract covering such vehicle less the unearned portion of the finance charge with respect thereto and less the salvage value of such vehicle
- With respect to a vehicle damaged by fire prior to repossession, for which the Dealer had submitted to the lending institution acceptable evidence of vehicle insurance at the time the contract was purchased covering the same, but the insurance had been voided without the Dealer's knowledge or control, or had expired by its terms: the amount of any loss or damage that would have been covered by the insurance if it had remained in effect at the date of the loss, plus the amount of the deductible, if any, that would have been applicable under the insurance, less the first $1,000
- With respect to a vehicle damaged by collision prior to repossession, for which the Dealer had submitted acceptable evidence of vehicle insurance at the time the contract was purchased covering the same, but the insurance had been voided without the Dealer's knowledge or control, or had expired by its terms: the amount of loss or damage that would be covered by insurance if it had remained in effect at the date of the loss, plus, for each collision in connection with which the resulting damage exceeded the deductible which would have been applicable under the insurance, the amount of the deductible not in excess of $500 per collision.

The repurchase price to the Dealer for each contract covering a medium or heavy commercial vehicle repossessed by the lending institution and returned to the Dealer shall be calculated on the same basis as for a light commercial vehicle except for:

- If it is returned to the Dealer after the redelivery period, the repurchase price to the Dealer will be the "as-is" value of such vehicle at the time of repossession, plus accumulated unpaid late charges and all expenses of retaking and repairing the vehicle to effect repossession in the manner described above.

Exceptions to Limitations on Dealer's Responsibility

The Dealer unconditionally guarantees and remains fully responsible for repurchasing, upon demand, for the full amount remaining unpaid for:

- Any retail installment contract assigned to the lending institution on a full guaranty basis
- Any retail installment contract (irrespective of the form of assignment):
    - With respect to which there has been a breach on any of the Dealer's representations and warranties to the lending institution, as set forth in such agreement
    - With respect to which there has been a breach of any of the Dealer's representations, warranties and obligation to the retail customer thereunder
    - With respect to which any material misrepresentations were made in the transaction details or the credit application process that were relied on by the lending institution in its decision to purchase the contract without regard to the Dealer's knowledge or lack of knowledge of such misrepresentations

- Evidencing the sale of a vehicle more than eight model years old (in Arkansas, more than four model years old) at the time of the sale

Limited Repurchase Plan

In most states, the finance institution will purchase certain contracts from the Dealer on a limited repurchase (recourse) basis. Contracts eligible for purchase on this basis are generally those covering passenger cars and light commercial vehicles (16,000 lbs. GVW or less) and medium and heavy commercial vehicles (over 16,000 lbs. GVW).

The Dealer's responsibility for contracts assigned on a limited repurchase basis is the same as it is for contracts assigned on a repurchase basis (except that the redelivery period with respect to medium and heavy commercial vehicles is 120 days) until the customer pays the lending institution:

- Each of the first 24 installments coming due on an equal consecutive monthly payment contract
- Each of the installments coming due within the first 24 months on contracts written on terms other than equal consecutive monthly payments
- If the vehicle is a medium or heavy commercial vehicle, one-half of scheduled installments

Thereafter, the assignment of that contract becomes "without recourse" to the Dealer except as follows:

The Dealer remains responsible for a pro-rata portion of any refund paid or credited to the retail customer (in accordance with "Refunds for Anticipated Contracts") and, to the extent of the unearned portion of the rate of differential paid or credited to the Dealer on that contract, for the amount of any net loss sustained by the lending institution in connection with a defaulted contract.

Contract Purchase Price

Lending institutions purchase acceptable retail installment contracts from the Dealer at discount rates established from time to time by the lender with the Dealer. The lending institution pays or credits the Dealer the total of payments of each contract purchased less the discount charge and any payments that the lender may make for, or on behalf of, the Dealer for insurance or otherwise. The amount so payable to the Dealer is known as "Dealer Proceeds." The lender may withhold a portion of the Dealer Proceeds as security for all of the Dealer's obligations to the lender and its subsidiaries or affiliated companies. In the case of a manufacturer's lending divisions, this would include the parent company and any subsidiary insurance companies owned by the manufacturer. Periodically, the lender pays the Dealer (without interest) the amount by which the sum in the Dealer Proceeds Withheld account exceeds a specific amount. If the Dealer substantially discontinues submitting contracts to the lending institution for purchase, the lender may discontinue payment of the excess in the Dealer's Proceeds Withheld account until all the Dealer's obligations to the lender and its subsidiaries or affiliated companies have been paid in full, including debit balances created by refunds for anticipated contracts and charge-backs as described in the section, "Refunds for Anticipated Contracts," found under Dealer Reserve.

The following is an example illustrating a typical sales transaction and finance contract purchase by the lender. In this example, the Dealer obtains the balance of the selling price by selling the contract to the lending institution. If the contract is sold to the lender for less that the face amount, it is said to be discounted.

Finance Contract Computation
Cents Omitted

Customer Retail Price	$18,500
Sales Tax*	925
License and Title	120
Customer Cost	$ 19,545
Less Down Payment	- 995
	$ 18,550
Less Trade-in	8,000
Customer Credit Advance	$10,550 (Contract in Transit)
Finance Rate (APR) Per Year	12%
4 Years	48
Finance Charge	2,785
Total Finance Contract	$13,335

When the contract is received by the lender, the Dealer is either credited or wire transferred $10,550 and customer pays monthly payments directly to the lender.

$$\text{Monthly Payment} \qquad \frac{\$13,335}{48} = \$277.82$$

*Sales Tax computed based on 5% tax rate times Retail Price $18,500. In some states, sales tax is computed on the difference between Retail Price and Trade-in, or $18,500 - $8,000 = $10,500 X .05 = $525

NOTE: In some states the customer can purchase comprehensive insurance and add it on to the credit advance (unpaid balance) and payments. Also buyers can purchase Package Insurance (Credit Life, Disability, Extended Service Contracts and others). In these cases, the amount of the total insurance cost is then added to the amount of credit advanced and monthly payments.

The Dealer will sell the foregoing contract with the finance institution for $13,335 and in this way would collect the balance due on the sale of the car.

Dealer Reserves

When the Dealer is successful in securing the financing of a retail sale, the Dealer is usually paid for this service; commonly called Finance Reserve. Finance reserve compensates the Dealer for selling the finance plan, and also for preparing the customer's statement and the conditional sales contract or chattel mortgage. If the Dealer also assumes the responsibility for repurchasing repossessed vehicles, as under the repurchase plan, the amount of the reserve paid by the finance institution is increased. In states where it is legally permissible, the Dealer can further add income from installment sales when insurance is sold as part of the finance contract.

Motor vehicle sales finance legislation enacted in some states regulates Dealer reserves which may be paid as a result of some sales. In almost all states, the competitive environment assures Dealers that major lending institutions will offer similar rates and reserves. Differences in finance plans generally exist only in the various services offered to the dealer and it's customers.

Income from Dealer reserves is one of the most important sources of dealership profit. When combined with the sale of insurance or other aftermarket products, finance reserve and commissions from insurance products often make the difference between making a profit (for the total dealership), or perhaps, losing money. For this reason it is *imperative* that the Dealer maintain close control of all finance business created by the dealership.

Dealer reserves are generally computed by a discount rate. This is basically the rate charged to the Dealer who then marks up that rate to the consumer, e.g., the lender charges the Dealer 10% (discount rate) and the Dealer charges the customer 12%.   However, many lending institutions will pay a flat fee for the sale of contracts, particularly those that are discounted to the consumer as an incentive to stimulate new business. Others offer various bonus plans based on the percent of Dealer finance business (penetration) that a particular lending institution receives.   In those instances, the lending institution might offer an additional 1/2% to 1% reserve if the dealership finances 60% or more of their finance business with that lender. Still others will offer volume bonuses. When the Dealer reaches a certain dollar or contract volume, the bonus becomes effective.

The Dealer and business manager should always be aware of which lending institution offers the most favorable and *consistent* reserve plans. Caution should be exercised when the Dealer is approached by a new lending institution offering more competitive reserves. In these cases, the lender may offer a more favorable reserve, but will not service the Dealer in the most beneficial way. Often, longevity and allegiance with a particular lender or lenders will provide a greater long-term return then that of one offering a limited-time special reserve structure. The business environment of the late seventies and early eighties provides an excellent example. In the late seventies, dozens of lenders crawled out of the woodwork, vigorously seeking Dealer finance business. Many succeeded by offering significant reserve structures as compared to those who had been servicing Dealers for many years. When interest rates soared in the early eighties (prime rates in excess of 20%) these lenders either went away or in many cases, actually began charging the Dealer to accept finance contracts.

Reserves are typically paid to the Dealer on a monthly basis, less any charge-backs. Charge backs are those reserves paid to the Dealer that were reduced because the consumer paid the contract off early, defaulted on the contract, or had the vehicle repossessed. The Dealer will receive a statement from the bank showing all contracts purchased, the reserve earned, and any charge-back amounts (see Refunds for Anticipated Contracts below). The following is an example, taken from the earlier finance example, of a finance reserve based on a discount method:

Basis: The customer was charged 12% on a finance balance of $10,550, with a total interest charge of $2,785. The discount rate in this example is 10% (cents omitted).

Finance Charge to the Consumer	$2,785
Less Finance Charge Computed at Discount	$2,293
Dealer Reserve	$ 492

It's important to note that the difference between the discount rate and the final rate charged to the consumer varies considerably. These variations may include:

- The competitive environment
- State usury laws (the discount rate might be 11%, but the state's usury rule caps the rate at 12%)
- Type of finance plan, e.g., without-recourse, with-recourse or limited recourse

Refunds for Anticipated Contracts

In most cases, the lending institution discount charge will be less than the finance charge made by the Dealer to the customer. In this event, the difference between these charges (know as "Rate Differential") will be a part of the Dealer Proceeds and will be paid or credited to the Dealer. The rate differential may, at the lender's option, be determined by the annual percentage rate ratio method or any other reasonable method. In the event the contract is paid in full before maturity, the lender will pay or credit to the customer a refund of the unearned finance charges. The refund will be calculated on the customer's total finance charge, less any applicable acquisition fee. Unless otherwise agreed, the Dealer is responsible to the lender for the pro-rata portion of the refund that is applicable to the rate differential paid or credited to the Dealer on the contract.

Retail Financing Rates

Most, if not all states have enacted legislation covering the retail installment of sales of automobiles and other durable goods. These laws frequently establish the maximum finance charges permitted by a lending institution operating within the state. Laws affecting finance charges are called Usury Laws. These laws place a maximum cap on the interest rate that can be charged.

The actual customer rates which are in effect in any particular state generally depend both on the usury laws in that state and the competitive environment which prevails. Rates for financing of used cars are typically higher than new car rates because of the greater risk of default.

Finance charges are computed by simple interest calculation, based on the unpaid balance and is identified as Annual Percentage Rate (APR). Because most finance rate calculations are computed on the unpaid balance, the following is a simple example of the interest calculation, based on the unpaid balance for the first five months of the contract:

__Basis:__   Amount Financed: $10,550.00, APR: 12%
Months Financed: 48, Monthly Payment: $277.82
Contract Date: January 1, First payment due February 1

Date of Payment	Days of Interest Computed	Principal Payment	Interest Payment	Outstanding Balance
January 1				$10,550.00
February 1	31 days	$169.32	$108.50	$10,380.68
March 1	28 days	$182.34	$ 95.48	$10,198.34
April 1	30 days	$177.32	$100.50	$10,021.02
May 1	30 days	$178.82	$ 99.00	$ 9,842.20

The above example demonstrates how the outstanding balance is reduced through principal payments. As the contract matures, principal payments increase, while interest payments decrease.

A Dealer may enter into an agreement with a finance company to pay the finance company an amount to cover the difference in the finance company's "buy rate" and the APR charged in order to provide below market retail rates to customers. This procedure is called a "buy down." Legal council should be sought regarding state laws that may govern the use of "buy downs."

Insurance

Few investments made by the average consumer today are greater than that of a new or even used vehicle. Most new vehicle prices today top $18,000, with many falling into the $25,000 to $35,000 range. The fact that most individuals purchase their vehicles with borrowed funds, makes it obvious that insurance is needed to cover this investment. Such insurance certainly isn't just limited to those who finance their vehicle purchase. Consumers who make their purchase with or without the use of borrowed funds rarely can afford risking the loss of their investment caused by an accident, theft or other means.

As previously noted, where state law permits, the automobile Dealer may sell insurance as part of the sale of the vehicle. In this case, a portion of the premium is paid to the Dealer along with the finance reserve. In some states, the Dealer may become what is known as a direct agent of the insurance company. In those instances, the Dealer earns additional profits even from cash sales when physical damage insurance is sold to the customer. Furthermore, like any insurance agent, the Dealer may also profit from insurance renewal business when the original policies expire.

As a side benefit to vehicle insurance, the selling Dealer quite often retains repair business resulting from insurance losses. The Dealer values the customer and wants to see him or her continue to enjoy the car as a result of quality repairs. Obviously the Dealer's service, body shop and parts departments profit.

From a pure protection standpoint, the customer, the Dealer and the finance institution are all concerned with insurance. Most, if not all, lending institutions require specified minimum levels of insurance, and require the Dealer to verify that the insurance coverage is in place at the time of vehicle delivery. The coverages most often required are collision and comprehensive coverage, and liability protection. Collision coverage normally includes a $50, $100, $250 or $500 deductible, and covers the vehicle for accidents that may occur. Most insurance policies waive the deductible if the insured driver is involved in an accident where he or she is not 50% or more at fault. Comprehensive coverage gives protection against virtually all damage other than collision and includes fire, theft, vandalism, glass breakage and many other common perils. The customer may provide their own insurance coverage through an agent of choice, or they may secure it through the Dealer or finance institution, where legal. Liability coverage includes protection for the insured against law suits, or injury resulting from an accident.

Credit life and disability insurance are typical offerings as part of a finance contract. Credit life provides for the payment of the balance due (on the finance contract) in the event of the death of the customer. The premium for such coverage may be included in the contract balance. Disability coverage involves making the customer's monthly finance payment in the event he or she becomes disabled. Such payments continue until the customer is able to return to work.

Caution should be exercised in the area of credit insurance. Some states do not permit an automobile Dealer to sell credit insurance. Others restrict prices as well as commissions earned. Credit insurance has also come under vigorous attack from various consumer advocate groups. Much of this was brought about by unfair and deceptive selling practices of some Dealers. In those instances, huge profits were made from the sale of credit insurance and some Dealers sacrificed sound business judgment when selling these forms of insurance's, for the sake of exorbitant profits.

Truth-In-Lending

The Consumer Credit Protection Act (Federal Law) was enacted by the federal government to protect consumers who finance their purchases of consumer goods and services. It basically requires any company in the business of extending credit, to provide accurate information about the cost of such credit. This law was intended to:

- Prevent any deceptive practices relating to the actual cost of the credit obtained
- Provide consumers with accurate information that they can use to compare financing options
- Protect consumers against discrimination in the extension of credit

The Consumer Credit Protection Act includes three major sections: Truth in Lending (Regulation Z, Consumer Leasing (Regulation M) and Equal Credit Opportunity (Regulation B).

<u>Truth in Lending (Regulation Z):</u> contains specific provisions requiring disclosure of relevant finance information, to the customer. These include:

- The amount financed
- The amount of the finance charges
- The annual percentage rate (APR) used in calculating the finance charge
- The payment schedule, including the number of monthly payments, amounts, and due dates of payments
- The total of payments
- The demand for payment feature, if any
- The total sale price, i.e., the sum of the cash price, other amounts financed not part of the finance charge, and the finance charge itself
- The prepayment penalty, if any
- The late payment penalty, if any
- Insurance requirements

<u>Consumer Leasing (Regulation M):</u> similar to Truth in Lending, requires disclosure of relevant information such as:

- Amount of lease payment and when due
- Total of lease payment
- Insurance requirements
- Late charges
- Mileage limits, including excess mileage charges
- Any liabilities of the lessee at termination including residual value (if an open-ended lease) and any excess wear and tear charges

<u>Equal Credit Opportunity (Regulation B):</u> prohibits discrimination against race, religion, national origin, sex, marital status, age, alimony or if the applicant is on public assistance. Limitations also include certain questions that cannot be asked on a credit application. Any applicant for credit must be notified

within 30 days of application as to the credit decision. If the decision is a denial, a written statement of the reasons must be provided, if requested.

If the Dealer advertises credit or lease terms there are certain disclosures that are required be published. They include:

<u>Finance</u>

- Amount of or percentage of down payment
- Amount of any payment
- Number of payments or period of repayment
- Dollar amount of any finance charge
- The applicable annual percentage rate
- Total of payments

<u>Lease</u>

- Amount and number of payments
- Total of payments ,
- Capitalized cost reduction, if any
- Mileage limits and any excess charges
- Amount due at lease inception i.e., first months' lease payment, security deposit, license, title and taxes, or any other amounts due at delivery

The Dealer must also make certain that these regulations are adhered to. Penalties for non-compliance are extensive. If there is any question regarding these various laws, the Dealer should seek advise from legal council. Particular note should be made of the fact that the law specifically excludes any liability on the advertising media itself for violations of the credit advertising provisions.

Summary

This chapter covered the evolution of installment credit, including the different types of financing available to automobile Dealers. It also covered the basics of rate computation, and the importance finance income has on the dealership's profitability, including the sale of aftermarket insurance products.

CHAPTER 7

CHAPTER VII

INSURANCE

Introduction

In analyzing insurance for automobile dealerships, three types of losses should be taken into consideration:

- Catastrophic loss due to fire, windstorm, hail, flood and natural disasters, often called Peril Insurance. This would apply to building facilities, contents and auto inventory.
- Large economic losses caused by lawsuits brought against the company through negligence and other legal actions relating to injury or property damage.
- Other losses such as theft, vandalism, minor physical damage, dishonesty, pilferage, etc.

Any astute automobile Dealer, or any businessperson, would never think of opening their doors without adequate insurance, covering every area where they may be held liable. In some states, various statutes make certain coverages a requirement. Essentially, it is simply good business practice to be protected against financial disaster which might befall the dealership business.

The dealership's business manager is frequently entrusted with the responsibility for determining the need and securing adequate coverage at a minimum of cost. This should always be done with the approval of the Dealer. The business manager should have a good understanding of the types of policies a dealership generally requires, what coverage each policy provides, and what specific exclusions or limitations they contain.

Except for life and health policies, most insurance policies have four similar parts:

Declarations: The Declarations contain information given to the company when the policy was initiated. This information includes the dealership name and address. It also lists the dates of the policy, term of the policy, the coverages purchased including the premium charges for each, limit of insurance, and the maximum payment for claims the company will make under each coverage.

Insuring Agreement: The insuring agreement is the company's promise to pay. It lists the occurrences the company agrees to cover.

Exclusions: Exclusions show which situations are outside of the scope of protection provided by the insurance agreement. Some perils or occurrences are not covered. However, other exclusions still retain limited coverage for specific circumstances. ***Exclusions should be carefully read from beginning to end*** by both the business manager and the Dealer principal.   This review should take into account any exceptions that might be important to the dealership and it's operation.   All too often, Dealers find out the realities of exclusions after the loss, when it's too late.

Policies generally contain exclusions simply because some risks are uninsurable. For example, injury or damage you cause intentionally is excluded, it is a deliberate act. Insurance is designed to cover only those events which might or might not occur. Some perils or risks are better insured by other policies specifically designed to do that job. In addition, some risks are just too large to insure, such as a nuclear event. Those with unique exposures can usually buy an endorsement for an additional charge to cover their special needs.

Conditions: Conditions spell out the rights and duties of the company and the insured with respect to claims, premium payments, termination of contract, etc. Some define the dealership's responsibilities after a loss. If these responsibilities are not met, the policy might not pay for the loss claimed.

DEALER'S INSURANCE GUIDE - Coverages

The information presented in the "Dealer's Insurance Guide" section was prepared for dealerships by Universal Underwriters Insurance Company in cooperation with the Michigan Automobile Dealers Association.

The purpose of insurance, generally stated, is to stand between the policyholder and financial disaster. Therefore, the importance of a properly arranged business insurance program cannot be overstated. While no two Dealerships are alike, some standard recommendations are practical. The rest are guidelines to consider.

The cost of insurance is a substantial overhead item and is directly related to the frequency and severity of accidents, injuries, and other occurrences resulting in insurance payment. With those two thoughts in mind, it is important to know that a properly arranged, comprehensive insurance program, with all avoidable overlaps and gaps eliminated, may cost no more than an uncoordinated and perhaps inadequate program.

It is strongly recommended that the owner(s) participate personally in the selection of the insurance representative, in all discussions of the insurance coverages, and that they make themselves available for periodic reviews of the operations with the same representative. Since no dealership operates in exactly the same way, a review of insurance coverage at intervals is vitally important. Any change in the Dealership operation can potentially affect the coverage provided or needed by the policies.

Insured Dealers consider their insurance representatives in the same way that they do their lawyers, accountants or other professional advisers. A qualified insurance representative charged with the professional responsibility of arranging the program and keeping it in proper order deserves this consideration and will insist upon it. Types of insurance include:

PROPERTY

Building Insurance

If the dealership or any of its owners own the building in which the dealership operations are conducted, there is a need for adequate building insurance. Buildings are normally insured by extended coverage against the perils of fire, vandalism, and malicious mischief.

It is not always easy to determine the actual insurable value of buildings. If the property is relatively new, valuation may not be difficult, but in the case of the older property, the most reliable index to the insurable or replacement cost of the property is obtained by the use of an appraisal by a qualified appraiser or contractor. Where an appraisal is performed, care should be taken that the uninsurable portions of the building (land, foundations, footings, and some paved areas) be excluded in arriving at the insurable value since these portions of the building are normally not subject to insurance.

It should be obvious that the depreciated book value of the property should not be used for insurance purposes. Neither should the original purchase price be used, because these values would not be accurate.

There is the option to insure buildings at the replacement cost rather than the sound insurable or actual cash value. This option, when elected, would require larger amounts of insurance, but settlement of the loss would be based upon the replacement cost at the time of the loss rather than the depreciated or actual cash value of the property.

Where the property covered by the policy is subject to any mortgage, the name of the mortgagee should be indicated in the policy in a mortgage clause acceptable to the mortgagee. Likewise, if there is more than one insurance policy covering the property, great care should be taken to be certain that they are identical in the application to loss.

Contents Insurance

Contents insurance applies to personal property contained in buildings occupied by the dealership and includes parts and accessory inventories, furniture and fixtures, machinery and equipment, personal effects, and leasehold improvements and betterments. The word contents in the insurance parlance does not include automobiles since these are special types of property insured in special ways.

Contents values are normally insured by extended coverage against the perils of fire, vandalism and malicious mischief and, if the building is equipped with automatic sprinkler system, against sprinkler leakage damage. (Coverage applicable to contents from robbery, burglary, etc., is discussed separately.)

If there is any substantial amount of variation in the inventory of parts and accessories during the period of a year, a monthly reporting form policy is recommended. This policy requires a monthly report of values to the insurance company with the values reported being based upon an actual cash value, i.e., replacement cost less depreciation.

Business Interruption

Most automobile Dealers would be subject to heavy loss if a fire or other insurable peril caused a substantial shut-down or interruption of the operations. This is particularly true with respect to the sale of service and parts. Some dealerships can set up temporary arrangements to continue a portion of the business, particularly the sales of vehicles, but it would be virtually impossible to continue a profitable service and parts business if the building were destroyed.

There are many forms of business interruption or business suspension coverage, but its primary purpose is to protect the dealership against loss of earnings caused by destruction or damage to the premises from the perils of fire and extended coverage. It is not practical in this presentation to outline all the various forms and their application to specific cases but, here again is an illustration of the necessity for a dealership representative to determine exactly which of the several forms available will most adequately protect.

Plate Glass Coverage

Most automobile dealerships have substantial investments in plate glass installation or occupy buildings where these installations are present. Glass coverage includes accidental breakage to the glass specifically described in the policy. The policy also provides a basis for recovery of the cost of repairing or replacing frames and sashes and the cost of temporary installations or boarding up where that is necessary. There is some unavoidable overlap between the plate glass policy and fire and extended coverage policies. The principal overlap results because both policies cover the glass for windstorm and certain other named perils.

Plate glass insurance will be needed if the lease requires the dealership to insure plate glass breakage. In those cases it is also important that the plate glass policy be written in accordance with the conditions of the lease - that is, that the proper insured be named in the policy. Sometimes the lease specifies only that the glass be insured and other leases specify that it must be in the name of the building owner.

Plate glass insurance policies must include a list of the plates to be covered. Accurate measurements are necessary. The policy coverage is on a replacement cost basis. The problem of riots has created a distressing loss situation on plate glass. The Dealer is well advised to think of small size plates upon replacement when ordering in an area subject to riot exposure.

Boiler and Machinery Insurance

If a boiler is on the premises, it is imperative that boiler insurance be carried, because only under a boiler policy can insurance be obtained against the loss from explosion of the boiler.

An important feature of boiler and machinery insurance is the thorough inspection service given by the insurance company to its policyholders to make certain that the insured objects ate in good mechanical and operating condition. Any condition which needs attention is promptly submitted to the insured so that necessary repairs may be made in the interest of accident prevention.

CRIME

Employee Dishonesty Loss

The franchised automobile Dealer is particularly subject to losses traceable to the dishonesty of employees. When one considers the number of ways in which an employee or two, or more employees working together can take advantage of an automobile Dealer's situation, the use of a fidelity bond is urgently recommended. Blanket fidelity coverage can be arranged so that all employees are covered. The cost of this coverage is directly based upon the number and type of employees engaged in the dealership operation.

Robbery and Burglary Insurance

Property owned by automobile dealerships is subject to loss or damage from burglars, robbers, and other dishonest acts. There is a wide assortment of policies available.

Open stock burglary insurance protects merchandise, furniture and fixtures, and equipment against loss by burglary when the premises are not open for business. One of the conditions which must be present before recovery can be made is visible signs of forcible entry on the exterior of the premises. An optional endorsement can waive this requirement, which would broaden the coverage

Money and Securities Policy

It is recommended that a broad form money and securities policy be purchased. This covers messengers both to and from banks. It also includes coverage for money left overnight in the dealership.

INVENTORY

Vehicle Inventory Insurance

Dealers are already aware of the necessity to insure the value of their automobile inventory. All new and used automobiles and trucks, including Dealer-owned demonstrators, should be covered. This would include vehicles held for sale, cars used in repair and demonstrator service, and the dealership interest in consigned vehicles. Vehicles which are floor planned must be covered subject to the requirements of the floor plan finance agreement.

The policy most frequently used is the automobile Dealer's monthly reporting form policy which requires the Dealer to report each month the full insurable value of all vehicle included in the insurance. Coverage on the vehicle reporting form policy includes fire, transportation, theft, vandalism and malicious mischief, and the Dealer's supplemental coverage. This latter includes windstorm, hail, earthquake, explosion, smoke from heating equipment, riot and civil commotion, aircraft, floor or rising water, and water damage (except rain, snow or sleet). Collision coverage is an option as is coverage for false pretense losses sometimes called trick and device insurance. The theft coverage included in the basic policy also includes pilferage from insured automobiles subject to a deductible.

It is important for the Dealer to realize that the full reporting clause in the policy requires that a monthly report of inventory be submitted and that this inventory report be accurate and represent the full insurable value of the vehicles being covered by the policy. Failure to submit reports on time or in the proper amount can seriously impair the Dealer's ability to recover any losses in full. The individual charged (usually the business manager) with the preparation of these monthly reports should be carefully instructed by the insurance representative.

If floor-plan-financed units or other-financed vehicles are to be included in the policy protection, the necessary and acceptable loss payable clause in favor of the lender must be attached to the policy. In nearly every instance, the lending organization (the bank, finance company, etc.) will require the original policy or certified copy of the policy be in its possession.

GARAGE LIABILITY

Garage Liability Coverage

The garage liability policy is a public liability policy specifically designed to protect automobile sales and service agencies. Its application will be considered specifically to the franchised automobile Dealer. This coverage is perhaps the most vital to the Dealer's protection.

The garage liability policy (not to be confused with garage keeper's legal liability insurance) provides protection for liability, bodily injury and property damage imposed upon the dealership by law. Coverage is provided for the premises at all locations, garage operations (service, parts and body shop operations and new and used vehicle sales), and the ownership, maintenance and operations of dealership vehicles.

The coverage provided for the use of automobiles is frequently misunderstood. The policy provides coverage (subject to the exclusions described below) for the "ownership, maintenance, or use of any automobile for the purpose of garage operations, and occasional use for other business purposes, and the use for nonbusiness purposes for any automobile owned by or in charge of the dealership, and used principally in the dealership operations." Coverage is also provided for the ownership, maintenance, or use of any automobile owned by the dealership named in the policy while furnished for the use of (1) the named insured, a partner therein, an executive officer therof, or, if a resident of the same household, the spouse of any of these, or (2) any other person or organization to whom the named also extends to cover automobiles not owned or hired by the Dealer such automobile is neither owned nor hired by the named insured, a partner therein, or a member of the same household of any such persons."

This is a complicated and sometimes misunderstood paragraph in the policy. The policy has been directly quoted and this quotation serves to illustrate the necessity for consultation with the insurance representative as to the coverage actually provided. As to who is insured, the garage liability policy extends protection to any officer, employee, director, or stockholder while acting within the scope of their duties, and to any person or organization legally responsible for the use of an automobile covered by the policy, provided such use is with the permission of the dealership and the automobile is used within the scope of such permission. The garage liability policy does not protect any officer, employee, director, or stockholder, or any other person while operating an automobile owned by him or her, or a member of his or her household. This is an extremely important provision, frequently overlooked, since it indicates that the garage liability policy does not extend to protect a salesperson who owns their own demonstrator. This would be equally true of officers or partners in those cases where the individual officer or partner owns the automobile which he or she is driving.

There are a number of major exclusions in the policy which restrict or limit the coverage and sometimes eliminate the insurance altogether.

First, the policy does not apply to any automobile rented to others, except service rentals. Automobiles being operated in the prearranged or organized racing or speed contests are not covered nor are haulaway trucks, tank trucks, tank trailers or any automobiles used therewith.

There is an endorsement entitled "Limited Coverage for Certain Insureds" which is available in most states. When this endorsement is attached to the garage liability policy, it normally will resort in a premium savings without a reduction in coverage. Its effect is to make the coverage contingent rather than primary with the respect to dealership customers or prospective customers while driving dealership automobiles. The endorsement when attached, does not in any way reduce or restrict the coverage for the insured dealership. However, it does to a large degree, make the customer's own insurance responsible for their own protection.

In the garage liability coverage, automobile Dealers are protected for product liability. This coverage in the garage liability insurance is not a separate policy but is built in as a rider with the other terms and conditions of the insurance contract. Dealers are protected for liability allegedly caused by defective workmanship in the manufacture, servicing or repairing of motor vehicles. The policy usually contains a feature which applies a deductible to claims resulting from defective workmanship as they apply to the customer's automobile. There is provision to eliminate this deductible for a nominal additional premium.

In the basic garage liability policy, there is no coverage for property damage to products sold, handled or distributed by the insured Dealer, and this would extend to and include both new and used vehicles. **The various possible areas of misunderstanding in this part of the coverage are so numerous** as to require a very careful consultation with the insurance company representative.

The garage liability policy, like all other liability policies, contains a supplementary provision to the effect that the insurance company will defend its policyholder against any suit for damages even if such charges are false and completely groundless. However, that agreement to defend is contingent upon the allegation or the claims being covered by the policy. This is a long way from saying that the insurer will defend regardless of the nature of the claim and this provision is also frequently misinterpreted by policyholders.

Garage Keepers Legal Liability

Garage Keepers Legal Liability policy covers the dealership's legal liability for loss or damage to vehicles left in the care, custody, or control of the Dealer. (Garage Liability policy does not cover this and there is often confusion due to the similarity of the policy names.)

The intent of the policy is to protect the Dealer when the dealership is clearly negligent and therefore liable. If the dealership is not negligent, the customer's own insurance policy applies. Also, this policy generally does not cover theft of personal property left in the vehicle by the customer unless the entire automobile is stolen.

Fire Legal Liability

To those Dealers operating in buildings or at locations which they do not own, Fire Legal Liability insurance is extremely important. The Garage Liability policy does not protect the dealership for any claim arising from property which is in their care, custody, or control, nor does it apply to real estate which he occupies under a lease or rental agreement. Therefore, it is important that a study be made of the exposure to which the Dealer is subject in the lease or rental agreement governing the use of the rented property. It is also possible to ask the landlord to provide the tenant with an endorsement naming him or her as an additional insured on the landlord's policy.

MISCELLANEOUS COVERAGES

Umbrella Policy

It is common practice for dealerships to arrange for umbrella protection which provides liability insurance over and above the basic liability protection at minimal cost. This form of excess or high limit legal liability coverage should be considered as a valuable addition to the dealership's overall insurance program.

The umbrella's purpose is to install on top of the basic liability coverage an additional layer of protection with limits up to one million dollars, and often several millions of dollars.

The umbrella coverage can give virtual assurance that liability coverage will be adequate. Since these policies are not now uniform, the Dealer should make certain that he or she understands the policy they are buying and its application.

There is a provision for "retention of loss" by the policyholder on claims which are not subject to coverage in the underlying insurance. This is another way of saying that a deductible applies, and since these amounts of retention or deductibles can be substantial, this provision needs to be very clearly understood.

Workmen's Compensation Insurance

Every automobile Dealership can be considered a proper subject for workmen's compensation insurance.

The workmen's compensation policy is standard in form and covers the Dealer's statutory liability under the state's workmen's compensation law. Coverage is mandatory for all employers having three or more employees and provides for the payment of benefits to or on behalf of employees injured in the course of employment. The coverage applies to hospital, medical expenses and weekly compensation as stipulated by the workmen's compensation law of the state.

Leased Car Coverage

The statement has already been made that the basic garage liability policy does not extend to cover leased car or rental car operations. Where the dealership is engaged in either or both of these activities, it is necessary that additional coverage be arranged, not only for the customer's protection but for the dealership itself. This statement is likewise true in the event that the dealership's leased car or rental operations are conducted by a separate corporation or firm. Since there are many different approaches, let us suffice here to say that **coverage needs to be arranged separately and with great care** since it is not provided in the basic liability protection provided by the garage liability.

Host Coverage

Host coverage can be an extremely important provision, as it protects the dealership from liability claims arising from persons who were served alcoholic beverages. Host provisions generally apply to alcohol consumed on the premise or served on be-half of (paid for by the dealership) the dealership at an off-site location. This coverage would cover employees and non employees of the dealership.

This review of the insurance coverage, a necessity for all dealerships, has emphasized the value of a coordinated insurance program for the dealership and has provided a description of the policies which are essential if the dealership is to be protected. The intent of such review is not to make the business manager an insurance expert but to give him or her a basis for intelligent exploration with the Dealer's selected insurance representative. These two should determine what coverage is best for that dealership from the standpoint of both adequacy and minimum cost. It is the responsibility of the business manager, working in consultation with the insurance representative, to secure coordinated, adequate insurance program.

In addition to the insurance suggested in the "Dealer's Insurance Guide," there are a number of miscellaneous policies which may be applicable in certain instances. Included are such coverages as:

- Accounts receivables
- Valuable papers
- Owners' contingent liability
- Dealer's personal umbrella
- Non-garage operations
- Advertising liability
- Employee benefits liability
- Discrimination, harassment, wrongful termination liability
- Depositors forgery
- Punitive damage liability

The application of these insurance policies to the individual dealership is a matter for discussion between the business manager and the insurance representative.

SELECTION OF AN INSURANCE REPRESENTATIVE

Insurance representation generally falls into three broad categories (agent, broker, and consultant). A description and brief discussion of each follows, but the reader is reminded that these are functional relationships; i.e., one individual could be in two or more classifications depending on state law:

Insurance Agent

An insurance agent is defined as "a representative of the insurer in negotiating, servicing or effecting insurance contracts; he or she may be an independent contractor or an employee." An "independent" insurance agent usually represents several insurance companies whereas a "captive" agent or an insurance company employee usually represents only one insurance company.

Insurance Broker

An insurance broker is "a representative of the insured in placing insurance with carriers, but paid a commission by the insurer." In many jurisdictions, he or she is legally the agent of the insurer for collection of premiums or delivery of policies." The courts have generally held that since he or she does not represent the insurance company, but rather his client, they have a higher degree of responsibility to the insured. Some insurance brokers are also insurance consultants.

Insurance Consultant

An insurance consultant may not be licensed to transact insurance with an insurer. The consultant may function as an advisor to the public. There are a number insurance consultants whose sole function is providing advice on coverages and sources of purchase of insurance protection. The consultant is compensated by a fee charged to the client. A client must secure the services of a broker or an agent to purchase insurance protection.

Often the important question is what is the relationship between your representative and the company that issues your policy. Who pays the commission of fee? In considering two policies, what is his or her commission structure or compensation on each?

It is recommended that the Dealer review the following before considering cost in the process of selecting a representative:

1. His or her understanding of the automobile Dealer's business. This demonstrates to the Dealer the representative's competence to recognize the hazards of the industry that require protection. A car Dealer's business is a complex one and constantly changing. It requires an insurance representative to be close to the industry and sensitive to legislative and other coverage requirement changes. The Dealer may contact other car Dealers in the area that are represented by insurance representatives to gain further insight as to his or her overall performance. However, caution should be exercised in comparing rates or costs with the other Dealers because different dealerships may have different coverages or different rating plans.

2. What are the services that are offered. Services should include but not necessarily be limited to:
- A study of the risks and hazards of the Dealership.
- A review of current coverage and recommended improvements for protection.
- A proposal of premium costs and rates. Specifications of coverage must be carefully outlined by the insurance representative.
- A review of written policies at the time of delivery with the Dealer. The Dealer must be satisfied that he or she received what was ordered. It also provides the Dealer with the additional opportunity to understand the dealership's coverages thoroughly.

3. The representative's license status and business reputation. Insurance could be the difference between the success or failure of a Dealership. For that reason, the Dealer must do everything possible to insure that they are dealing with parties that are above reproach not only legally, but morally.

4. The insurance company or companies' financial and claims ratings. "Best Insurance Reports" published annually by A.M. Best Company, Inc., has been called the Dun and Bradstreet of the insurance business. This volume may be found in the possession of the insurance representatives, insurance companies and in the business section of most public libraries. They rate an insurance company based on the following principle factors:
- Good underwriting
- Economy of management
- Adequate reserves to pay losses & net resources for shock losses
- Sound investments

The final rating is based on "surplus to policyholders," continued or technical services of equities in unearned premiums, and loss reserves. The ratings are scaled ranging from $25,000,000 or more - AAA down to $250,000 or less - CC.

In addition to the financial rating, Best's rates the insurance company on their ability to respond to the needs of the policyholder based on a scale ranging from A+ (excellent) to C (fair). This correctly points out "many smaller companies are carefully and efficiently managed, and in sound proportion to the liabilities assumed."

After an investigation of several companies the Dealer should have at least two possibilities that are differentiated by their knowledge of the business, their services offered, and their cost. The choice of an insurance company is not necessarily based upon its size but on its overall ability to relate with the public.

Insurance Check List

An insurance advisor (agent, broker, consultant) should be able to recommend a complete insurance program for an automobile Dealership. This program would include not only complete protection from all public liability claims, but also losses that may occur in the operation of the business that would endanger profitability and permanency. In order to review the needs of the business in the area of insurance coverage, we have developed the following Insurance Coverage Check List that the Business Manager or Dealer can use to determine insurance voids and a list of insurable items that will be useful in discussing the total program with an insurance advisor.

INSURANCE LIABILITY CHECK LIST

	NEEDS	HAS	RECOM-MENDED	COMMENTS - DATES
I. PROPERTY LOSS				
Building				
Contents:				
Merchandise				
Furniture and fixtures				
Equipment				
Property away from premises (tools and equipment)				
Improvements and betterments				
Boiler & machinery/air conditioning				
Signs				
Plate glass				
II. CRIME				
Employee dishonesty				
Robbery on/off premises				
Safe Burglary				
Theft (Mechanical & Equipment)				
Counterfeiting				
Depositors Forgery				
III. INVENTORY/AUTO				
Owned vehicles				
Non-owned				
Hired cars				
Uninsured motorists				
Collision/comprehensive				
Garagekeepers legal				
Personal injury protection Statutory, excess				
Property protection, statutory				
IV. GENERAL LIABILITY				
Premises, operations - Comprehensive				
Products completed operations				
Independent contractors				
Contractual				
Personal injury liability				
Professional liability				

	NEEDS	HAS	RECOM- MENDED	COMMENTS - DATES
IV. GENERAL LIABILITY Cont.				
Liquor Law Liability				
Umbrella				
Aircraft/Watercraft				
Fire Legal Liability				
Water Damage Legal Liability				
Elevator Collision				
Workers Compensation All States Endorsement				
Longshoreman & Harbor Workers				
Medical Payments Coverages				
Extended Liability Endorsement				
Foreign Products Direct or Indirect				
V. OPERATING RISKS				
Loss of Income				
Extended Period of Indemnity				
Extra Expense				
Rent/Rental Income				
Contingent Business Interruption				
Property of Others				
Accounts Receivable				
Valuable Papers				
Data Processing Equipment or Media				
Transportation (Cargo)				
Leasehold Interest				
Surety: (License/Permits/Bonds/Others)				
IV. LIFE AND HEALTH				
Life				
Hospitalization				
Disability Income				
Key Man				
Employee: Life/Major Medical Disability Income				
Buy Sell Agreements				
Group Life				
Pensions				

Additional Insurance Terms

Actual Cash Value: Insures your property for an amount equal to the cost of repairing or replacing the damaged property with that of like kind or quality, or the cost of replacing your property less a reasonable deduction for wear and tear and depreciation.

Additional Coverage: This endorsement extends your policy to include loss or damage to your property by vandalism, sprinkler leakage, falling objects, weight of snow, ice, or sleet, collapse and premises burglary or robbery.

All-Risk: Your property is insured for "all risk" of loss or damage from any exterior cause with certain exceptions. Common exceptions are enforcement of a local ordinance, flood, back-up of sewers, depreciation, wear and tear, theft, and mysterious disappearance.

Burglary: The taking of property from within the premises by a person while the business is closed and there are visible signs of forcible entry into the premises.

Co-Insurance: A requirement in the policy that you agree to carry a specified percentage of insurance in relation to the value of the property at the time of loss. Failure to do so means you will not collect fully for partial losses.

Extended Coverage: This endorsement extends your policy to include loss or damage to your property by windstorm, hail, explosion, riot, riot attending a strike, civil commotion, aircraft, vehicles, and smoke.

Optional Perils: This endorsement extends your policy to include loss or damage to your property by falling objects, weight of snow, ice, or sleet, water damage, collapse, and breakage of glass.

Personal Injury: This endorsement extends your normal Bodily Injury Liability to include sums you are legally obligated to pay as a result of false arrest, libel, slander, and wrongful entry or eviction.

Replacement Cost: Insures your property for the cost of replacing your damaged property (new for old) with no deduction or depreciation.

Robbery: The taking of property by violence or threat of violence from a messenger or custodian, either on or off premises.

Sprinkler Leakage: Covers loss resulting from direct damage by leakage or discharge of water from an automatic sprinkler system or caused by fall or collapse of tanks which are part of such systems.

Theft: The broadest form of crime coverage: defined as any act of stealing or unlawful taking of property.

CHAPTER 8

CHAPTER VIII

ANALYZING AND INTERPRETING THE FINANCIAL STATEMENT

INTRODUCTION - ANALYSIS

Before the accounting cycle can be completed, all the journals must be posted to the ledgers, trial balances made, schedules summaries made of unit inventories, accounts receivables, accounts payables, etc. Once this is accomplished, the most important operating document in business, the Financial Statement (often called the operating statement), is prepared, completing the accounting cycle. From the information on the Financial Statement, the Business Manager can then make an analysis of the business. This analysis will make it possible for the Dealer to make intelligent decisions, based on facts, regarding the third step in business management - the **correction of out-of-line conditions.**

Analysis is the breaking down of the whole into small parts for the purpose of examining those parts relative to their relationships and importance to the whole. Almost analogous to analysis of the statement is it's interpretation - what does it mean? What does the analysis explain? How does it translate into knowledgeable information that is usable?

The workbook is the core of this chapter. From this detailed analysis of the statement, certain relationships and performance measures emerge, indicating the relative status of the total business activity. The computations in the workbook are detailed, and they cover the entire Financial Statement: total dealership analysis and evaluation, review of each section of the statement, plus departmental profit analysis. Completing each of these computations will provide a better understanding of the statement and the interpretation of the information contained therein. This chapter will focus on the generalized idea - the "big picture" of statement analysis and interpretation.

GENERAL CONCEPTS OF ANALYSIS AND PERFORMANCE MEASURES

Everything in life and business life is relative. We are happy or unhappy, tall or short, efficient or inefficient, profitable or less profitable in relation to or in comparison with something. For example: A person born in poverty does not know that he or she is poor - all those around them are poor - until the person sees and compares with more affluent people. In the business world this type of comparison is also true. A business may be making a profit and the principals in the business think that it's adequate. However, that profit may be much below the average profit made by others, indicating mediocre performance.

It is extremely important to understand how common it is for businesses to become lax during "boom" economic times. During these times, it becomes easy to fall prey to the bad habits such as reduced attention to sales and lax overall expense control. Even more important is the knowledge that, capitalizing on "boom" times can often mean the ability to survive during the cyclical downturns, so common to the automotive industry.

In the business world, numerous different items are compared to demonstrate relative performance. For example: Measuring performance may be done through trend comparisons that show if a situation is improving or worsening. Other measurements evaluate relative performance, including:

1. Performance this month vs. previous month
2. Performance year-to-date vs. year-to-date previous year or previous years
3. Performance this month vs. average month performance year-to-date this year
4. Performance this month vs. average month in previous year
5. Performance this month vs. same month previous year
6. Performance this month vs. objective (forecast) this month
7. Performance this month and year-to-date vs. Dealer composites or local or national   Dealer averages
8. Statement-to-statement comparisons to other Dealers as 20-Dealer group comparisons
9. Market penetration this month vs. market penetration year-to-date this year
10. Market penetration year-to-date this year vs. market penetration last year

When analyzing a statement, the comparisons in the first eight items listed above can be used for any section or account in the total dealership operation or for any department - by the profit centering concept, or for any computation derived from the statement. Ratios, percentages, and other computations from the statement can be compared in the first eight items above. For example: Percent return on investment, net profit as a percent of sales, break even point, cost of selling, liquidity ratios, solvency ratios, etc.

There are two types of standards of performance used to evaluate data.

- Internal standards: These are the standards that result from comparisons against what was done in previous periods, and secondly the performance against objectives. These are measured in the first six items listed on the previous page.

- External Standards: These are standards that result from comparisons to factors outside the dealership operation, including other Dealers, the manufacturer or distributor guides or objectives, Dealer area market penetration, Dealer composites, other Dealer statements such as Twenty-Group meetings.

External guidelines can be extremely helpful in interpreting the results of statement analysis. Sometimes these guidelines take the form of industry goals or objectives such as grossing 9% on new vehicle sales, grossing 50% of service and parts sales or 2% net profit to total sales. Sometimes these kinds of guides are not absolute -- the guide of 30-45-days supply of used cars does not mean that all used cars in inventory must be 30 days old, only that the total inventory should average 30-45 days. However, overpriced, poorly selected trades, or "stale" merchandise may bring the average over 30 days and thus become a problem. The use of any standard will depend on the understanding of it as it relates to individual dealership experience. Guides focus attention on a particular segment of the operation so that more detailed analyses may be made for the purpose of correcting out-of-line conditions.

Care must be exercised when using other Dealer or certain industry comparisons. They should be made to others of a reasonable size and geographic comparison. It would not be prudent to compare financial results of a Dealer located in a major metropolitan area who sells 3,000 new units annually to that of another selling 400 and located in an outlying community.

Ratios and Percentages

Financial comparisons are made easier through the use of ratios and percentages. They are particularly valuable when comparing other businesses that may be different in size or geographic location. Additionally, disclosure of sensitive financial data is eliminated through the use of these methods of comparison.

Some ratios can be expressed in reverse order. For example: Liabilities to Net Worth may be expressed as .7 to 1, or Net Worth to Liabilities as 1.4 to 1. Either case is correct. Ratios and percentages make comparisons easier and relevant.

The first step in analysis of the financial statement is to determine the relative strengths and weaknesses of the total dealership operation. In the workbook, this total dealership analysis includes the following format:

- Probability Analysis: Illuminates the varied methods of computing profitability. The most important reason for a Dealer to be in business is to make a satisfactory profit. These computations are listed as number one priority for that reason.
- The next most important item to consider is the determination of liquidity - the capability of rapid conversion to cash.
- Solvency of a business is critically important. It demonstrates the capacity to pay all debts. In particular, it indicates the long-term borrowing capacity and permanency of the operation.
- Efficiency comparisons show the computations that indicate the overall efficiency of management in directing the operation.
- Expense analysis of the total dealership could well be the difference between an acceptable net profit and ROI, or financial failure. The results of the expense control function, or lack of control, are ascertained through this expense analysis.

The second step is an analysis of Cash Flow. Cash Flow analysis is basically an examination of the balance sheet accounts. Cash flow by definition is the movement of trends among all the balance sheet accounts which increase or decrease the flow of cash.

Decrease in cash flow is indicated by (including examples):

1. Increase in assets: Purchase of used cars at the auction
2. Decrease in liabilities: Payment of parts open account

Increase in cash flow is indicated by:

1. Increases in liability and net worth: Placed owner's bonus into accrued liabilities account
2. Decreases in assets: Receipt of factory incentive receivables

Forecasting all the balance sheet accounts for the future is a means of determining cash needs. A comparison of month's supply of cash and working capital vs. guide is a quick way to determine the cash situation at a particular moment. If these two items are at acceptable levels there should not be a cash problem, especially if inventories are within acceptable limits and the expense structure is not excessive.

CASH FLOW FORECAST

_____________THROUGH__________

		MONTH	
CASH RECEIPTS			
VARIABLE & FIXED SALES			
FINANCE INCOME			
OTHER INCOME AND DEDUCTIONS (EXCLUDING FINANCE INCOME AND ADJUSTMENTS FOR DOUBTFUL ACCOUNTS)			
NEW VEHICLE HOLDBACK			
SALES OF SECURITIES FIXED AND OTHER ASSETS			
MISC. NOTES & ACCOUNTS RECEIVABLE			
TOTAL CASH RECEIPTS			
CASH DISBURSEMENTS			
NOTES PAYABLE - NEW VEHICLES & DEMOS			
NOTES PAYABLE - L&R UNITS			
DIRECT COST - L&R UNITS (EXCLUDING DEPRECIATION)			
PURCHASES - P & A AND OTHER INVENTORIES			
VARIABLE SELLING EXPENSES			
COMPENSATION - TECHNICIANS			
TOTAL FIXED OVERHEAD EXPENSES (EXCLUDING PREPAID & ACCRUED ITEMS AND DEPRECIATION & AMORTIZATIONS			
PREPAID AND ACCRUED EXPENSES			
BONUSES			
DIVIDENDS OR WITHDRAWALS			
PURCHASES OF SECURITIES FIXED AND OTHER ASSETS			
INCOME TAXES			
PRINCIPAL PAYMENT ON NOTES OTHER THAN VEHICLES			
MISCELLANEOUS DISBURSEMENTS			
TOTAL CASH DISBURSEMENTS			
TOTAL CASH & CONTRACTS - BEGINNING PERIOD			
NET CASH FLOW			
TOTAL CASH & CONTRACTS - END OF PERIOD			

The third step in analyzing the statement is profit centering -- the analysis of the departmental profit and loss items, including gross profit analysis.

The principal reason for this analysis is to ascertain in depth the strengths and weaknesses of the dealership operation. This analysis also highlights the weaknesses that must be corrected in the third step of the business management function. Listed below are generalized steps in correcting or improving the business operation.

- Provide an accurate and consistent accounting system - know where you are and where you have been!
    - Is your accounting staff well trained
    - Do you have effective accounting processes in place, and are they well communicated
    - If the dealership's computer system up-to-date

- Increase Sales Volume:
    - Increase employee productivity and efficiency. Train, then motivate and recognize through incentives that reward performance
    - Maintain effective customer relations and owner retention activities
    - Advertise, market (sales promotion) and merchandise more efficiently. Carefully plan these efforts with all departments. Planning must also include sufficient budget allocation, and built-in methods of promotion that track the accountability of dollars spent.

- Increase gross profits on what you do sell:
    - Improve selling techniques
    - Understand current used car values
    - Devise pay plans that reward gross profit efficiency (do not undermine customer satisfaction efforts through pay plans rewarding excessive gross)
    - Continuously review sales and service pricing policies with departmental management

- Decrease expenses
    - Establish budgetary control
    - Assign responsibility
    - Follow-up
    - Review and change compensation plan, where appropriate
    - Continually review staffing needs and adjust accordingly
    - Implement an employee suggestion system and reward those who contribute

- Turn inventory faster
    - Are managers trained in inventory management (Used Car, New Car, New Truck and Parts Managers)

- Replace ineffective employees - hire well
    - Are departmental managers trained in the area of hiring, training and motivating employees

- Maintain an effective daily operating control
    - Is this activity maintained **all** the time, or just during poor economic times

The following page includes a diagram of the various items that have been discussed (general terms) thus far.

The end result of all analysis is useless if actions are not taken to improve profitability. Financial analysis cannot replace good judgment. There should be no reluctance to make changes. However, change just for change's sake, can prove an exercise in mental gymnastics if not well thought out as to sound business judgment. The old adage, "nothing ventured - nothing gained" is true today. If management never changes anything there is no growth and profits suffer. The statement analysis provides the necessary information (tools) -- the action taken and their results is the payoff.

In addition to judgment and past experience involving corrective actions, there are a number of other items to consider that result from financial analysis. Information —supplied by your banker, department head, distributor, factory representatives or consultant – may also be a key ingredient in the analysis and interpretation process. Corrective actions may involve business management analysis in many other contexts. Changing procedures is a constant and daily activity. The business management contribution to the process can vary considerably. However, it should always be present, but never completely dominate. It is **one important** tool of management. The third and final step of business analysis - the corrective phase - is the point at which financial analysis blends with every other management tool.

Dealership Operations Analysis

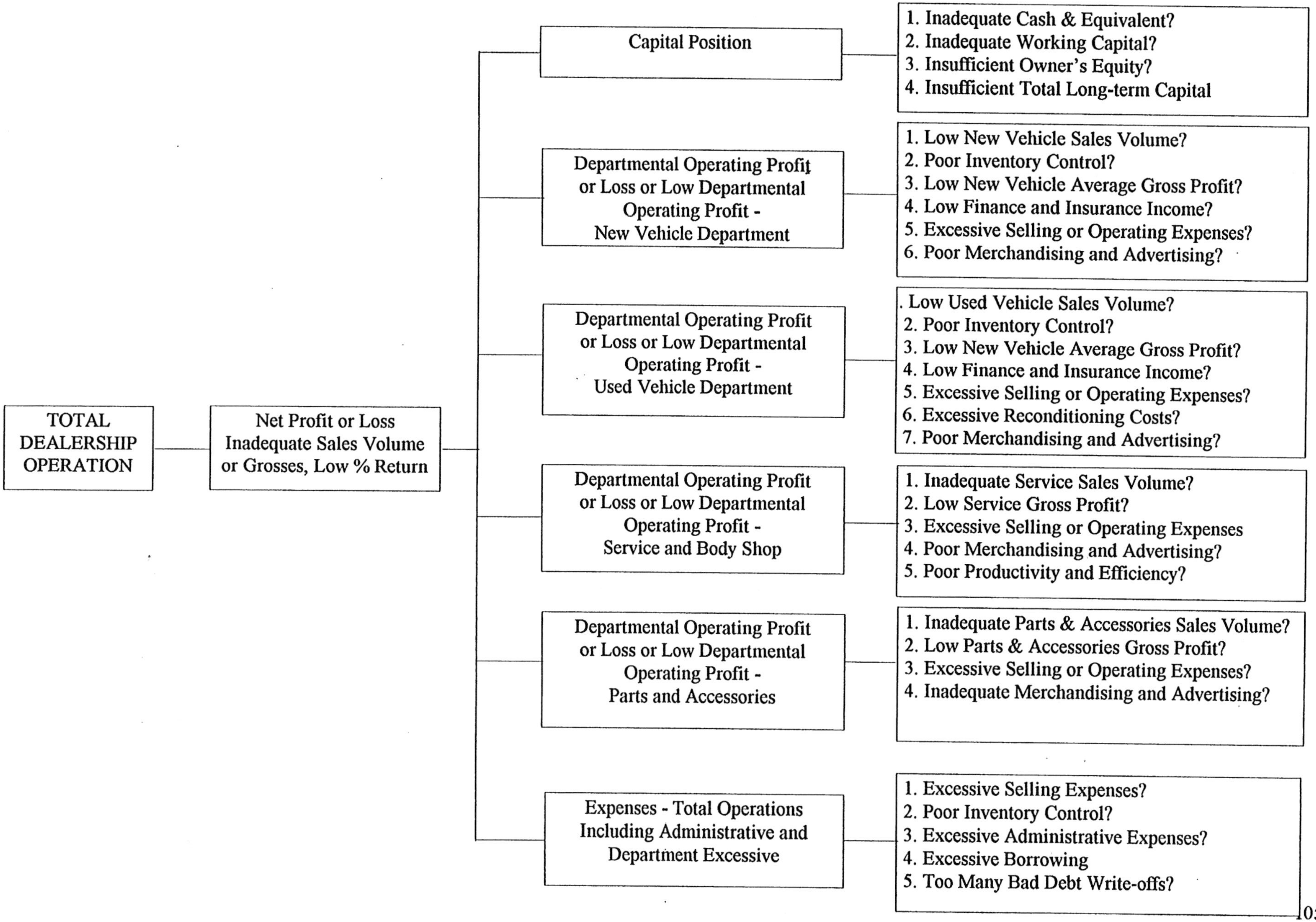

TOTAL DEALERSHIP OPERATION → **Net Profit or Loss Inadequate Sales Volume or Grosses, Low % Return** branches to:

Capital Position

1. Inadequate Cash & Equivalent?
2. Inadequate Working Capital?
3. Insufficient Owner's Equity?
4. Insufficient Total Long-term Capital

Departmental Operating Profit or Loss or Low Departmental Operating Profit - New Vehicle Department

1. Low New Vehicle Sales Volume?
2. Poor Inventory Control?
3. Low New Vehicle Average Gross Profit?
4. Low Finance and Insurance Income?
5. Excessive Selling or Operating Expenses?
6. Poor Merchandising and Advertising?

Departmental Operating Profit or Loss or Low Departmental Operating Profit - Used Vehicle Department

1. Low Used Vehicle Sales Volume?
2. Poor Inventory Control?
3. Low New Vehicle Average Gross Profit?
4. Low Finance and Insurance Income?
5. Excessive Selling or Operating Expenses?
6. Excessive Reconditioning Costs?
7. Poor Merchandising and Advertising?

Departmental Operating Profit or Loss or Low Departmental Operating Profit - Service and Body Shop

1. Inadequate Service Sales Volume?
2. Low Service Gross Profit?
3. Excessive Selling or Operating Expenses
4. Poor Merchandising and Advertising?
5. Poor Productivity and Efficiency?

Departmental Operating Profit or Loss or Low Departmental Operating Profit - Parts and Accessories

1. Inadequate Parts & Accessories Sales Volume?
2. Low Parts & Accessories Gross Profit?
3. Excessive Selling or Operating Expenses?
4. Inadequate Merchandising and Advertising?

Expenses - Total Operations Including Administrative and Department Excessive

1. Excessive Selling Expenses?
2. Poor Inventory Control?
3. Excessive Administrative Expenses?
4. Excessive Borrowing
5. Too Many Bad Debt Write-offs?

CHAPTER 9

CHAPTER IX

FORECASTING

Forecasting Rationale

Forecasting: Why forecast? Why go through an exercise in the prediction of future sales, profits or expenses? The answer lies in what the forecasts are used for. Forecasts are important because they are used when setting objectives for the future month or quarter. In most dealerships, forecasts are also made a year in advance, usually in late November or early December. The monthly forecasts are used predominately in the operation of the dealership. If forecasts are to be used in setting objectives, one could ask why objectives? The reason for setting departmental and dealership objectives are:

- They establish a target or goal for each individual to work toward. Without these goals or objectives, there is a lack of understanding of what is expected of a particular department manager, general manager, or other dealership employee(s).
- Objectives make performance evaluations, against what is expected, possible. Objectives establish acceptable levels of performance.
- They encourage managers to think about actions that must be taken to meet their objectives.
- Objectives help "weld" the organization together by making participants feel a part of the overall dealership management.
- They give the Dealer and department manager a chance to communicate their ideas and actions needed to meet objective levels.
- Objectives become a part of the Daily Operating Control (DOC). The DOC makes it possible to know if the manager is on target on a daily basis. They also make it possible to take remedial action to improve the situation before the month is over.

Without objectives, there is no final destination point for measuring progress.

Establishing Objectives

Establishing objectives is just as important as meeting them. Basic principles for establishing objectives include:

- Objectives must be set in a measurable way, and in writing. They must also be completed well in advance, and with the input of the person responsible for accomplishing the objective.
- Objectives must be reasonably obtainable. Unrealistically high objectives tend to negatively influence, and become wishes rather than objectives. Likewise, they must also be set at levels that stimulate improved performance.
- Objectives must be appropriate for the person held accountable. A department manager cannot be directly responsible for any objective he or she does not have direct control over.
- They must be followed and compared against performance on a regular basis, usually monthly. If objective accomplishments are not followed, they become mere numbers on a sheet of paper and are generally ineffective.

If month end variances are present, they should be reviewed with the individual responsible for accomplishment. At this review, reasons for missing the target must be ascertained. For example: If the parts gross profit objective is missed, and it is determined that parts sales on repair orders is the reason, then the parts manager must plan to correct that situation. That correction may include retail counter specials, parts and service seasonal promotions, advertising changes or increases, incentives, contests, etc. Whatever the decision, corrective measures must be developed and implemented.

There are many items to consider in establishing a forecast. A statistical review of past performance is necessary. Past performance, along with consideration of market trends, help provide the basis for estimating future performance. Generally, three years prior history is sufficient. However, in some geographic locations, five years may be more appropriate, particularly in areas that have experienced rapid expansion (homes and businesses) or significant economic depression.

The form shown on the following page is just one way to accumulate historical data for purposes of making forecast estimates. Note that a comparison can be made by a current month estimate to a three - year average, percent of past month, and a percent of the past three months. It is a matter of taking varied statistical relationships and arriving at a range within which the forecast month will fall.

In addition to past performance, there are other factors that must be considered prior to arriving at a final forecast. These include:

- Local economic trends (positive or negative)
- New legislation, federal and local mandates concerning the environment, worker safety, hiring practices and others
- Competitive activities, new Dealership(s) about to open nearby
- Special advertising or sales promotion activities already planned, including anticipated budgets
- Inventory availability, new and used, model discontinuance or new model entries
- Seasonal conditions, long-term (30-day) weather forecasts
- Availability of employees (vacations, illnesses, etc.)
- Taxation, increases or decreases in sales or other taxes

Historical Forecast Form

Sales

	19__	19__	19__	3 Year Total	3 Year Average Month	Current Year Forecast	Current Year Actual
January	85	79	96	260	87	91	89
February	90	83	104	277	92	97	98
March	102	103	113	318	106	116	119
April	120	117	133	370	123		
May	145	132	156	433	144		
June	140	129	163	432	144		
July	134	116	122	372	124		
August	106	102	118	326	109		
September	107	98	119	324	108		
October	143	136	154	433	144		
November	112	104	122	338	113		
December	94	85	103	282	94		
Year	1378	1284	1503	4165	1388		
Ave. Mo.	115	107	125	116	116		

Based on Three Year Average Month

	Each Month % of Year	Each Month % Previous Month	Each Month % Previous 3 Months
January	6.2	92.5	24.8
February	6.6	105.7	31.3
March	7.6	115.2	38.8
April	8.9	116.0	43.2
May	10.4	117.1	44.9
June	10.4	100.0	38.6
July	8.9	86.1	30.2
August	7.9	87.9	27.5
September	7.8	99.1	28.7
October	10.4	133.3	42.2
November	8.1	78.5	31.3
December	6.8	83.2	25.8
	100.0%		

The primary purpose of forecasts is to project and measure profitability of the dealership on a monthly basis. However, the forecasting process, particularly annual forecasting, assists the Dealer with major capital equipment, and building and facilities improvement planning. Key to any business's long-term success is it's ability to reinvest in the business through capital equipment and facilities. These are generally large expenditures not normally considered as typical monthly operating expenses. In some cases these capital expenditures generate immediate revenues, while others do not. Those that do not may include investments of appearance nature. Although appearance is extremely important, it is not easy to establish what direct impact appearance has on revenue.

Part of the annual forecast should include a "wish" list from each department manager. This list may include special shop equipment, expansion of the service department, parts department equipment or facilities needs, body shop equipment and additions, or special needs of the new or used vehicle operations. Lists should be divided by direct revenue generating items and those with no direct revenues. The lists should then be prioritized by essential needs, and those that can wait. The Dealer and Business Manager should then review the lists in light of anticipated profits and carefully select those capital expenditures within the dealership's financial means.

Forecasting and Daily Operating Control Procedures

As mentioned previously, many dealerships complete an annual forecast around the end of November or early December. From the annual forecast, the core monthly forecast (particularly fixed and semi-fixed expenses) can then be made simply by dividing the total by 12 months. Because every month's financial performance is different, particularly in the new and used vehicle departments, this core monthly forecast is adjusted based on historical data, then reviewed and update each month.

Approximately five days before the end of the month, a forecast meeting should be held by the Dealer and department managers to establish or adjust the next month's forecast, and to review status of current month results vs. objectives. Because the month-end Financial Statement would not be available at this time, a current DOC Statement should be used.

In preparation for the forecasting meeting, department managers should bring their forecasts for the future month, along with any other statistics or information that relates to the next month's business. This could include employee performance, advertising and promotional plans, and their own projections for next month's business. It is vitally important to have the managers participation in setting the final forecast -- they will be more meaningful and effective tools if this is done. After a review of each department manager's input, a final forecast is approved by the Dealer. This forecast becomes the objective for the Daily Operating Control. The Business Manager breaks the next month's objective down into daily working objectives, which are recorded on a DOC form. Actual results are then posted daily for each department by the business management or accounting department.

Daily Operating Control forms vary, depending on the level of detail the dealership wishes to track. Usually, the DOC tracks sales volumes, gross profits, expenses and net profit. As mentioned before, Dealers can make their own forms through the aid of today's more modern computer accounting systems and available software, or purchase forms from dealership supply sources. DOCs can be created to fit any particular dealership's needs.

Examples of other factors to consider in the Parts and Service Departments :

- How many productive mechanic stalls are available for selling service?
- Have any improvements been made since the last review of employee productivity and efficiency counter parts sales volume, internal parts and labor volume, and parts sales on Repair Orders?
- Are there any changes contemplated in operating plans or personnel?
- Has any new revenue-generating equipment been installed since the last forecast?
- Has any other new equipment or computer systems been installed that will help improve productivity?
- Are there any manufacturer parts or service specials being launched, including parts-ordering incentives during the next forecast period?

Discussions of these or other factors will aid in establishing more realistic Parts and Service Sales objectives. After these objectives have been established and agreed upon, the percentage of dollar sales and resulting gross profit is established, according to each individual type of sale. Again past performance should be considered, as well as any improvement factors that may be anticipated.

The percentages are then entered in the Parts and Service Sales Section of a Sales and Profits Forecast Form, and applied to dollar sales to arrive at total dollars of gross. A quick total of parts, accessories, labor and other miscellaneous shop profit can now be obtained. By deducting Total Overhead Expense from Parts and Service Gross, Net Operating Profit is obtained.

The Vehicle Gross section of the Sales and Profit Forecast Form is a projection of new and used unit sales and gross profits which the Vehicles Sales Managers agree can be reasonably expected. After agreement is reached on the number of sales expected for each line of vehicles carried by the dealership, they are posted in the appropriate place on the forecast. Vehicle Gross is then estimated. Past experience is generally relied upon heavily as a guide.

Like the Parts and Service department, factors affecting new and used vehicle sales and grosses should be considered, including:

- External factors beyond the control of the dealership such as a high grossing model being discontinued, slow arrival of new vehicle shipments, low volume of saleable used vehicles traded in, special Dealer Advertising Association-initiated sales, severe weather conditions and others.
- Internal factors resulting from poorly trained or motivated managers or salespeople, excessive internal labor charges, poor (out-of-market) appraisals, etc.

When the gross expected for each vehicle line is agreed upon, it is entered by vehicle line PNVS (Per New Vehicle Sold). Obtaining the total gross for each line then is a simple matter of multiplying the number of units by the gross.

The Used Vehicle forecast is the second part of the Vehicle Gross Section, and since the profitability of the Used Vehicle operation often determines the dealership's final profit, careful attention to this section must be given.

Many dealerships determine the availability of used units for sale by adding the expected inventory at the beginning of the month to the anticipated number of trade-ins on both new and used vehicles sold, plus any outside buying. Then decisions are made regarding how to gain maximum consumer activity on the lot, as well as what units to wholesale in order to maintain the desired inventory level and balance . Most Dealers plan for a 30- to 45-day turnover of used vehicles.

With the number of used unit sales and the average gross per unit determined, multiplying one by the other, as done with new vehicles, produces the total gross.

Finance Reserve Income is projected in the same manner, multiplying the per vehicle average by the number of vehicles which finance sales are expected (finance penetration) to be made. The result is included in the totals shown for vehicle gross and finance income.

By deducting variable sales expense from this total, variable net is obtained. This variable net, less operating cost obtained in the second section of the Sales and Profit Forecast, equals the expected operating profit.

A forecast arrived at in this manner, with the cooperation of the dealership's department managers, tends to be far more accurate than those is made without consulting the affected managers. Since the department managers themselves help set the objectives, there a greater effort to attain them, and it is the attaining of objectives which makes forecasting accurate.

Summary

This chapter has discussed the importance of setting objectives for overall dealership and departmental sales, expenses and profitability. Key is the need to establish these objectives, communicate them in writing, and follow through with their accomplishment, or lack of.

Departmental managers need to be involved in the setting of objectives, since they will be the responsible persons for meeting them. Their objectives must also be reasonable. Setting overly optimistic or unrealistic objectives can have a negative impact on actual performance.

CHAPTER 10

CHAPTER X

TECHNOLOGY

The Evolution of Computerized Management

Following World War II, the pace of business (and life in general) increased dramatically, contributing to increasing challenges in managing a Dealership efficiently. A lack of prompt and accurate management information was frequently a problem. In the late 1940s, virtually all Dealers managed their accounting and statement preparation manually. There sometimes were delays in getting the statement prepared, and human error was often the reason. Beginning in the 1950's and continuing on into the early 1960's, large main-frame computers became much more common, although they remained scarce and very expensive. Typically, they were owned by Computer Service Bureaus who developed standard sets of programs and used them to process their customer's service requests, usually accounting. One of the first of these service bureaus was the Controlomat Corporation in Boston, that did data processing for some of the larger Dealers in that city. Controlomat was later sold to Reynolds and Reynolds, a well known supplier of automotive forms and other dealership items. Reynolds and Reynolds refined the service bureau's equipment and offered computer services to Dealers on a national scale.

Basically the service bureau operation was simple. Their services to Dealers included:

- From source documents (new and used vehicle sales invoices, repair orders, cash receipts, checks, vouchers, purchase orders, etc.) accounting information was key-punched into a machine which produced machine-readable tape. The tape was then mailed to the service bureau.
- The Service Bureau ran the tapes through their computer to complete the accounting cycle. They prepared journals, ledgers, Trial Balances, Financial Statements and various Schedule Summaries. These reports were then mailed back to the Dealer.

By mid - 1960, thousands of dealerships were using Service Bureaus and computer makers. The largest of these were IBM, Burroughs, Honeywell, Sperry/Univac, and NCR. These early computers were very expensive to purchase and maintain. They were also very limited in their processing capabilities. For those Dealers who did buy a computer, most had to devise and program their own systems. As computers evolved, each succeeding increase in power was matched with lower prices. The advent of data transfer via telephone lines also increased flexibility. Taking advantage of batch services or off-line services provided the Dealer with the ability to tap into the main frame systems and receive "next-day" management information.

As the use of remote data transfer increased, so too did the ability to provide more complex and efficient computer services to the Dealer. During the '70s on-line services developed and marketed the capability to enter data at a terminal and retrieve that data on printers or terminals almost immediately. For the first time, a Dealer was able to access accounting data instantly and continuously. It was now possible to review certain portions of the general ledger, or recall an important management report at any time. Terminals located at the dealership were able to "talk" to computers located in other locations via common telephone lines. The on-line arrangement provided the Dealer the benefits of the computer, without the burden of investment in computer hardware, programming and associated maintenance. The cost of on-line service was based on data storage held by the computer and computer data storage capacity, and the duration of on-line access. The costs also included dedicated phone lines to handle transmission to and from the computer. These charges varied greatly and often increased proportionately with the distance from the host computer. Automated Data Processing (ADP) had come of age.

As computer technology expanded, and costs became more affordable, Dealers began purchasing computers for their own dealerships. The "in-house" ownership of the computer and associated software, terminals, cables, and printers, etc., offered many advantages, including:

- Greater number of programming options and increased processing speed
- Ability to "write off" depreciation of equipment
- Increased security associated with "In House" Computers

The Age of Personal Computers

Two of the most significant advances in computer technology have included the invention of the Personal Computer (PC) and the ability to integrate computer systems together. The PC evolved quickly, overtaking the main-frame and mini computers of the 1970s in processing speed, computing power and storage capacity. Computer systems integration has improved dealership business efficiency and reduced costs. For example: Previously, a billing clerk would complete the paperwork on the sale of a new or used vehicle, typically on one kind of computer. The accounting information: sales, cost of sales, licenses and taxes, still had to be re-entered on a different computer used for accounting. Systems now allow key accounting data to transfer directly from one computer to another, eliminating the need to enter data twice.

Computers have become an absolute necessity in today's automobile dealership. Hardware and software systems have been designed and made available for every department, covering virtually every operational part of the dealership. *Not only are computers important to the dealership operation, they will significantly change the way Dealers operate in the future.*

Even though computer system purchase is more affordable than ever before, it still represents a significant expenditure for the dealership. This is multiplied by added costs for computer-related equipment and software throughout the dealership. In the past, a dealership might only have a small mainframe-type system with one or two terminals. With modern PC systems, terminals are now often placed in many locations, and connected to the main or host computer. Additionally, obsolescence becomes a contributing factor in overall dealership computer costs. It's not unusual to replace an entire accounting system computer every five to eight years. Technology is changing so rapidly, new systems quickly evolve that are far superior and more productive than their predecessors.

Even though systems are expensive, and have to be replaced fairly often, newer systems generally deliver productivity increases sufficient enough to justify their cost.

The following includes a brief discussion on how computers affect various areas of the dealership.

<u>Accounting</u>

Increased accounting and inventory complexities are a "natural" for a computer to furnish up-to-date management data. With thousands of parts numbers to track or millions of dollars in vehicle inventory, only the combination of an advanced computer and efficient software can give the instantaneous updates necessary for tight inventory control. Computer systems furnish the information required to make sound business decisions. Tracking daily cash flow and managing expense control, profit analysis, etc., are only possible with computer assistance.

New types of computer software are now being developed and released that are commonly referred to as "Expert Business Systems." These systems actually read the financial statement and automatically make comparisons against previous performance, forecast and group composite data. They then alert the business manager or Dealer to problems or out-of-line conditions. In addition, this "smart" software identifies specific areas to look for the problem, and also provide recommended solutions. As these systems continue to evolve and improve, financial statement analysis will become more of a science than an art.

<u>Data Base Management</u>

Data base management is rapidly evolving as a key strategy to assist Dealers in developing new business and retaining existing customers. They enable dealerships to capture hundreds, even thousands of names and addresses of customers who visit their facilities. These include prospects for new or used vehicles, those who bought from the dealership, and service or body shop patrons. Powerful PCs can capture, sort in any conceivable configuration, and report on anything a customer has done with the dealership. PCs play a major part in supporting a dealership's marketing and promotional activities. Mastering the nuances of data base management will allow the Dealer to effectively communicate with it's customers.

<u>Inventory Control</u>

Just one manufacturer's line may include as many as 10, 15, or even 20 individual models. Differing trim levels offered on those models can exponentially increase the actual number of available combinations the dealership may have. Computers help managers with ordering and stocking of inventories. They can track key issues such as those models and equipment levels that are selling quickly and those that are not, including color, what's been in stock too long, and what's fresh. They can also help to predict at what time of year certain vehicles sell better than others. These types of information can be extremely valuable for forecasting inventory needs and placing orders with the factory. If inventories are managed effectively, floor plan interest can be cut substantially.

Vehicle locator systems are also important to both inventory control and the dealership's selling effort. These systems have improved dramatically over the years, and now quickly and efficiently provide inventory information. The continuous increase in computer performance has not been lost on the emerging used car "superstores." These highly automated used vehicle resellers depend on sophisticated computer systems to log inventory on a visual data base, complete with color graphics on each vehicle in inventory. They also are able to find vehicles using any combination of features, body styles, and other factors. These sophisticated used vehicle inventory computing systems are just one example of the growth of sophisticated computer management.

<u>Vehicle Specing</u>

The majority of Dealers still use "printed and bound" data books and vehicle ordering guides. However, these guides will soon become less prominent. Numerous computerized tools are available that provide salespeople with the ability to select models, equipment specifications, and colors directly through the aid of a computer. These "specing" programs have become very useful, particularly in specing commercial trucks. They take much of the guess work out of selecting the right equipment for the job, relying on a data base that matches vehicle specifications to buyers' individual needs. With the introduction of the laptop computer, salespeople can now take the specing program right to the customers' home or place of business. They can even link up via modem to the dealership's inventory database.

<u>F&I and Billing</u>

For many years, F&I departments have used computers to compile finance and lease payment information, as well as to complete the printing of contracts and other sales paperwork. As mentioned previously, F&I and billing systems are now integrated with the dealership's main accounting systems. Advances in systems and software have made F&I and billing operations considerably more efficient, particularly in regard to F&I. Various software packages allow the F&I manager to show detailed rate comparisons on finance contracts and leases to consumers. This helps them to make more intelligent decisions, and improves overall customer satisfaction. Many of these comparisons previously were impossible to calculate manually, or took too long.

Computers systems also facilitate instant communications with lending institutions. Credit applications can be transmitted in seconds and approvals, in many cases, are instantaneous.

<u>Service</u>

Computer technology in the service department has, perhaps, evolved more rapidly in recent years than any other department. Computers and their related technology affect service operations in many ways, including:

Computer diagnostics: Every vehicle made today is equipped with some type of on-board computerized engine management system. In some cases, only a specific diagnostic computer systems can diagnose a system condition. In other systems, a Compact Disc-Read Only Memory-based (CD-ROM) diagnostic system is used to detect, and then re-program, a computer PROM (also referred to as a chip) to repair the vehicle. This technology is advancing at a pace too rapid to even cover it's potential in this chapter.

Repair order generation: More sophisticated service operations have a built-in data base management system that contains all customer and vehicle information, including maintenance history. Inputting a customer's name or vehicle ID number (VIN) will allow access to the Dealer service data base. The service advisor can then review vehicle and customer service history and make intelligent recommendations about service needs. These systems are also able to print the customer repair order, and log the requested repair or maintenance operations into the service scheduling system.

Service Scheduling: As part of the integrated service system, computers assist the shop foreman or service scheduler by providing up-to-the-minute information regarding technician availability, work-in-process, pending work and scheduled appointments. This information is then used to make informed decisions pertaining to the scheduling of work, and can also notify service advisors of anticipated problems with scheduling of appointments or existing work. It also provides complex reporting of the service department's scheduling history, work-flow process and efficiencies.

Shop Manuals and Bulletins: To eliminate volumes of printed documents, shop manuals and factory bulletins are now being published on CD-ROMs. CD-ROM usage saves a considerable amount of money in printing costs. They also minimize the space required to store volumes of books at the dealership.

<u>Parts</u>

Parts department inventory benefited as one of the earliest applications of computer technology, and considerable advances have been underway ever since. Parts ordering and locator systems were the first computer-related systems to affect the parts department, and they have improved significantly over time. Today, inventory could not be efficiently managed without the aid of modern computer systems. Parts inventory systems can also be linked to the accounting system, eliminating the need for duplicate input. Computerized data bases published on CD-ROMs also began to replace printed parts catalogs. Thousands of pages of parts catalog information can now be stored on one small disc. CD-ROM catalogs are also able to supplement conventional printed data with pictures, cross-indexing and more flexible searching capabilities.

<u>Body Shop</u>

Just as CD-ROMs are revolutionizing the parts department, they are also having a major impact on the body shop. CD-ROM systems are replacing manuals used for estimating body repairs. Computer-based estimating systems allow body shop estimators to look at entire vehicle sub-systems and ensure that more complete repair estimates are completed. And, like the service department, repair orders can be generated and later stored in the service database system.

Other

Computers are now and will be used for numerous other applications in the future throughout the dealership. These include marketing and promotion, sales training, management training, product specifications, word processing, operations analysis and other applications.

Marketing and Promotion: Advances in PC power and speed, coupled with better document processing software, printers and enhanced data management capabilities are providing the tools dealerships need to develop many kinds of marketing communications. Today's laser printers make it possible to create professional-looking letters, announcements and brochures that can be sent to customers. By enabling dealerships to design their own promotional materials (rather than paying for such services at a local printer) relatively expensive computer equipment can pay for itself in a year or less.

The Internet is quickly becoming a valuable marketing and communications tool for U.S. and international businesses. Through an Internet Service Provider, Dealers can promote themselves in an area of the Internet called the World Wide Web. The World Wide Web can present graphical information to PCs equipped with a modem and special interpretive software. This rapidly growing area provides Dealers with a place to develop a "Home Page" or special signature graphic. The cost is fairly moderate, yet it enables a Dealer to reach millions of potential customers. Although most of the Internet audience will not be in the Dealer's general area, the cost may be worth reaching the few consumers that are. Internet usage by consumers is said to be growing at rates in excess of 100% annually.

Interactive marketing and communications tools are also becoming more common, and more sophisticated than ever. PC-based CD-ROM applications are being used as supplements to paper-based new vehicle catalogs, and as product information displays both in-dealership and at off-site locations. The reproduction and distribution of CDs amounts to only a fraction of the cost of printing catalogs and duplicating video tapes. Many manufacturers such as GM, Ford, Chrysler, Toyota and Mercedes Benz are committed to replacing all printed parts catalogs, product information displays and other materials with purely electronic interactive presentations by the year 2000.

General Communications

Computers systems and software have improved the capabilities of telephone systems and voice-mail, e-mail, satellite communications, interactive distance learning and other voice and data transmissions devices.

Telephone/Voice-Mail Systems

Telephone systems have seen tremendous advances over the last ten years. Today's system capabilities include in-bound and out-bound call volume tracking, computerized calling, voice-mail, automated response-type activities and caller-ID. For example: a customer can call the service department computer directly to find out the status of their vehicle. Another example would be after-hours voice-mail, allowing customers to specify a particular person or department, leaving a detailed message.

E-Mail

E-mail is quickly becoming a popular method of communication. For systems that are linked via Local Area Networks (LANs), electronic messages can be sent to each computer terminal on the LAN. E-mail can also be accessed and used through on-line services such as America-On-Line, Compuserve, Prodigy or through direct Internet access. With the launch of Windows '95 and Microsoft Net, more and more consumers will have direct access to the Internet, and be able to send and receive e-mail communications.

Satellite Communications

Satellite applications have expanded dramatically, and will continue to do so in the future. Many manufacturers have established satellite operations to facilitate data transmission with their Dealers, and to allow for in-dealership television programming and video communication. Satellite data transmission eliminates the need for telephone lines, and provides great savings to the Dealer.

Interactive Distance Learning

In tandem with satellite transmission, several facilities have been opened that facilitate interactive training and communications activities. Through these channels, dealership personnel can attend training without having to travel long distances. In a classroom setting, instructors communicate with the learners using video and often two-way audio. This enables learners in the audience to speak directly (live) with the instructor even though he or she might be hundreds of miles away.

Combining the PC's power with the distribution capability of satellite broadcast, led to the development of interactive teleconferencing. This powerful hybrid puts the user in control of the program. It provides the ability to respond to questions, and total responses instantaneously, displaying results to the entire learning audience.

Other Transmission Devices

There are numerous other computer-assisted applications in use at dealership's today. These include wire transfers in and out of the dealership's bank account, credit card transaction approvals, consumer credit applications, and others.

<u>A Look Into the Crystal Ball - the Future</u>

Computers will play an even greater role for the dealership of the future, including:

- Continuous improvement in the areas of data base management for tracking, communicating, and following up with customers
- Computers and software will continue to become easier to operate, more powerful and more effective
- Linkage between dealerships on a nationwide scale will become more prevalent (Already done in some parts of the country)
- Advances in "Expert Business Systems" software capabilities
- Improved communications with the factory
- Improvements in communications with finance sources and more paperless transactions
- Automobile display areas will be equipped with terminals to provide customers with on-the-spot vehicle options and pricing data
- Consumers will acquire pricing and vehicle availability information directly through the Internet, and will be able to place their order directly with their local Dealer via on-line
- Extended use of vehicle on-board computers, including electronic access to area maps or other traffic and road information

COMPUTER SELECTION AND EVALUATION

The automotive industry has experienced substantial growth and changes, particularly in the computer-related aspects of dealership operations. That growth has exacerbated sharp cost increases, exerting strong pressure on profitability.   This has led Dealers to new business methods to enhance efficiency and productivity, and thus increase profitability.

Before any decision is made with regard to purchasing a new "in-house" computer system or expanding an existing one, a thorough investigation should take place concerning costs versus benefits (ROI). Most dealerships could benefit by new or improved computer systems, but not every dealership can afford them.

Because there are so many different hardware and software systems available, our discussion will be limited to the dealership's accounting system computer.

When deciding on a new system, the following questions should be answered:

- Is the business manager or controller tied down with clerical (data input) functions such that he or she cannot effectively analyze and manage?
- How much and what kind of training will be needed? Where will the training take place?
- Will we have to replace, eliminate or add personnel?
- Is inaccuracy of information a problem for the dealership?
- Are required reports completed on time?
- Do department managers have sufficient and timely information to manage their departments?
- Is the Dealership hampered by a lack of information?
- Do you have your DOC before noon?
- Will increased speed improve accounting and other efficiencies in your operation?

Choosing a Computer

If there is a decision to purchase a new or expanded computer system, contact several companies who might fill your needs. Be certain that the companies contacted are approved by the manufacturer(s) of the line the dealership carries. There are only a few factory approved computer system vendors. Schedule an **ample** amount of time for each of the salespeople from the companies contacted for demonstration of their systems. Follow-up visits will most likely necessary. Systems do vary in their capabilities as do the services provided by the computer supplier -- do your homework.

Utilizing investigative techniques and reviewing all important considerations will help to insure a better "fitting" system. Most system providers (Reynolds and Reynolds, ADP, EDS and others) provide very detailed checklists that help to identify individual dealership computing needs. Take the time to carefully compete these check lists, and use them in the decision-making process.

Conversion

Before any computerized system is implemented, the business manager must make certain that all administrative and management personnel understand why the dealership is installing a new or expanded computer system. The right people should be properly trained by the systems representatives, and these people should follow all recommended procedures. Serious accounting or operational problems may result if installation procedures are not followed precisely.

If replacing an existing system, one system should be operating smoothly before the other is completely disconnected. Additionally, dealership records must be backed-up prior to installation. If incorrect data is put into the new system, incorrect reports will be the results.

Because of phenomenal growth within the computer industry, the number and variety of Dealer systems has increased considerably; new systems will become available even as this is being written. It is important, therefore, that the Dealer along with the business manager select the systems that meet their objectives, and from the right supplier. There is nothing worse than spending tens, even hundreds of thousands, on a system that doesn't do everything that you wanted it to do in the first place.

Storage and Security

Most computer systems incorporate routine back-up saves that take the information stored on the hard drive and transfer it to a disc or magnetic tape. This should be done at minimum every day. Backing up a system can save many hours of manual data input labor should a system failure occur. Additionally, media used for storage of back-up information can be invaluable when searching for archival data, particularly in the event of an audit. Back-up discs or magnetic tapes should be placed in a secured area. Obviously, sensitive dealership financial data is contained on these discs.

Most systems today can control access through the use identification codes. The various employees who use the computer system are provided access only to those areas they have clearance to enter. The Dealer, General manager or Business Manager may have full access, while a receivables clerk may only have access to payable and receivable data.

Summary

Numerous areas of existing and emerging technology have been covered in this chapter. Perhaps the best summary would include the statement that by the time this chapter is revised, printed and distributed, new technology will have already been developed. One of the most critical aspects of managing an automobile dealership(s) by the year 2000 will be the application of technology. Therefore, staying abreast of emerging technology will be critically important to the success of the Dealer's operation in the future. More important will be the ability to identify emerging technology, then understand how to apply it in the everyday operation of the dealership.

Dealership Statement Analysis

NADA
AUTOMOTIVE
EDUCATION
CENTER

 NORTHWOOD UNIVERSITY

TOTAL DEALERSHIP ANALYSIS
How Profitable Is Our Business?

I.   NET PROFIT MARGIN (RETURN ON NET SALES)

    A.   Formula:

        YTD Net Profit Before Taxes $__________

            Page No. __________   Line No. ____________

            Divided by: ÷

        Net Sales YTD $__________

            Page No. __________   Line No. ____________

        Equals: Return on Net Sales   __________%

II.   PERCENT RETURN ON INVESTMENT

    A.   Formula:

        Net Profit Before Taxes YTD $__________

            Page No. __________   Line No. ____________

        Divided by Sum of: ÷

        Common Stock $__________

            Page No. __________   Line No. ____________

        Retained Earnings $__________

            Page No. __________   Line No. ____________ $__________

        Equals % Return on Investment   __________%

III.   PERCENT RETURN ON OPERATING INVESTMENT

    A.   Formula:

        Net Profit Before Bonus And Taxes $__________

            Page No. __________   Line No. ____________

            Divided by: ÷

        Operating Investment [*] $__________

        Equals % Return on Operating Investment   __________%

---

[*] *Operating Investment is Working Capital plus (Fixed Assets less Land and Building.)*
All Formulas presume a 12 Month Statement.

TOTAL DEALERSHIP ANALYSIS
How Liquid Is Our Business?
(Capability of Rapid Conversion to Cash)

I.   **CURRENT RATIO**

    A.   Formula:

        Total Current Assets $________

            Page No. _______   *Line No.* _______

            Divided by: ÷

        Total Current Liabilities $________

            Page No. _______   *Line No.* _______

        Equals Current Ratio   _____ to _____

II.   **ACID RATIO** (QUICK RATIO)

    A.   Formula:

        <u>Total Current Assets less Inventories and Prepaids</u>
      Divided by Total Current Liabilities less Notes Payable New Vehicles

        Total Current Assets $________

            Page No. _______   *Line No.* _______

        Less sum of::

            Total Inventories $________

            Page No. _______   *Line No.* _______

                                        (+)   (-)

            Total Prepaids $________

            Page No. _______   *Line No.* _______

        Equals Current Assets less Inventories and Prepaids $________

            Current Liabilities $________

            Page No. _______   *Line No.* _______

        Less::

                                             ÷

            Notes Payable New Vehicles $________

            Page No. _______   *Line No.* _______

        Equals Current Liabilities less Notes Payable new Vehicles $________

        Equals Acid Ratio   _____ to _____

        The Acid Ratio indicates a firm's ability to take care of current
indebtedness without converting inventories - The Acid Test.

III. "WATCHDOG RATIO"

    A. Formula:

        Total Receivables $_________

                Page No. _________   *Line No.* ___________

                Divided by: ÷

        Accounts Payable $_________

              Page No. _________   *Line No.* ___________

        Equals "Watchdog" Ratio   _____to_____

TOTAL DEALERSHIP ANALYSIS
How Solvent Are We?
(Ability To Pay All Legal Debts)

I.   **DEBT TO OWNER EQUITY**

    A.   Formula:

        Total Liabilities $_________

              Page No. _________   *Line No.* ___________

              Divided by: $\div$

        Net Worth $_________

              Page No. _________   *Line No.* ___________

        Equals Solvency Ratio   ______ to _____

II.   **EQUITY TO ASSETS**

    A.   Formula:

        Net Worth $_________

              Page No. _________   *Line No.* ___________

              Divided by: $\div$

        Total Assets $_________

              Page No. _________   *Line No.* ___________

        Equals Solvency Ratio   ______ to _____

TOTAL DEALERSHIP ANALYSIS
How Efficient Is Our Business?

I.   PERSONNEL TURNOVER RATE

    A.   Formula:

        * Personnel Terminated YTD   __________

            Divided by : Average Personnel Employed

               Personnel Start of Year   __________

               Personnel End of Year   __________   ÷

                  TOTAL   __________

          Divide by 2 is average Personnel count during year   __________

          Equals Personnel Turnover Rate   __________%

---

* *Use the lower of Personnel hired or terminated. The lower of these two amounts represents employees terminated and replaced.*

How Efficient Is Our Business? (continued)

II. **BREAKEVEN POINT** (New Unit Sales Needed To Cover Unabsorbed Overhead)

    A.   Formula:

        1. Total Fixed Overhead YTD   \$__________

            Page No. __________   *Line No.* __________

            Service Dept. Gross Profit YTD   \$__________

            Page No. __________   *Line No.* __________

            Parts and Access. Dept. Gross
Profit YTD   \$__________   (-)

            Page No. __________   *Line No.* __________

            Body Shop Dept. YTD Gross Profit   \$__________

            Page No. __________   *Line No.* __________

        2. Total Fixed Gross Profit   \$__________

        3. Unabsorbed Overhead (Net Burden "Nut")   \$__________

            New Vehicle Gross Profit YTD   \$__________

            Page No. __________   *Line No.* __________

            Used Vehicle Gross Profit YTD   \$__________

            Page No. __________   *Line No.* __________

        4. Equals Total Variable Gross Profit   \$__________

            Less Total Variable Selling
Expenses YTD   \$__________   ÷

            Page No. __________   *Line No.* __________

        5. Equals Variable Net Profit   \$__________

            Divide by Number of New Units
Sold YTD   __________

            Page No. __________   *Line No.* __________   UNITS

        6. Equals Variable Net Profit per New Unit Sold   \$__________

        7. Divide Unabsorbed Overhead by Variable Net
Profit per New Unit Sold to obtain Breakeven
for year

                                       ____
                                       UNITS

        8. Divide by 12 to get Breakeven for Month

                                       ____
                                       UNITS

TOTAL DEALERSHIP ANALYSIS
BREAKEVEN POINT [*]

Procedure to determine New and Used Vehicle Sales needed to cover Unabsorbed Overhead

    A.   Formula:

1. Fixed Overhead Expense YTD $__________
   Page No. __________   Line No. __________

2. Gross Profit Service Dept. YTD $__________
   Page No. __________   Line No. __________

3. Gross Profit Part & Access. YTD $__________   (-)
   Page No. __________   Line No. __________

4. Gross Profit Body Shop YTD $__________
   Page No. __________   Line No. __________

5. Total Fixed Operations Gross Profit $__________

6. **Equals Unabsorbed Overhead (Net Burden, "Nut")** $__________
   (Gross profit needed from variable operations to Breakeven)

7. Divide by 12 to obtain Average Month Net Burden $__________

8. YTD Gross Per New Vehicle $__________
   Page No. __________   Line No. __________   (-)

9. Less YTD PNVR Variable Selling Expenses $__________
   Page No. __________   Line No. __________

10. Equals Retained Gross (Variable Net) PNVR YTD $__________

11. YTD Gross Per Used Vehicle Retailed $__________
    Page No. __________   Line No. __________   (-)

12. Less YTD PUVR Variable Selling Expenses $__________
    Page No. __________   Line No. __________

13. Equals Retained Gross (Variable Net) PUVR YTD $__________

14. New & Used Gross % of Total Variable Gross:

    % New Gross of Total Variable Gross   __________%

    % Used Gross of Total Variable Gross   __________%

15. Item 7 above X Item 14 (New) Divided by Item 10 above
    Equals Breakeven on New Per Average Month   __________UNIT

16. Item 7 above X Item 14 (Used) Divided by Item 13 above
    Equals Breakeven on Used Per Average Month   __________UNIT

17. **Total New And Used Breakeven Point Item 15 + 16.**   __________UNIT

---

[*] *This Excludes Wholesale U/V Gross and net additions and net deductions from Income.
New and Used Vehicle Gross includes Finance and Insurance Income.*

TOTAL DEALERSHIP EXPENSE ANALYSIS

I. TOTAL EXPENSES PERCENT OF SALES

    A. Formula:

Total Expenses, YTD $\$$__________
      Page No. __________   *Line No.* ____________

    Divided by: ÷

Total Sales, YTD $\$$__________
      Page No. __________   *Line No.* ____________

    Equals Total Expenses % of Total Sales   ___________ %

II. EMPLOYEE TO SUPERVISOR RATIO

    A. Formula:

Total number of Employees excluding Supervision   ___________

    Divided by: ÷

Total Supervisors   ___________

Employee per Supervisor   ___________

III. TOTAL EXPENSES PER WORKING DAY

    A. Formula:

Total Expenses, YTD $\$$__________
      Page No. __________   *Line No.* ____________

    Divided by: ÷

Yearly working days [*]   ___________

Equals Daily Expense Cost $\$$__________

---

[*] *(52 X 6 = 312 less six paid holidays)*

TOTAL DEALERSHIP CASH FLOW ANALYSIS

ASSETS

I. CASH MONTHS' SUPPLY OF CASH

    A. Formula:

        Cash And Contract $ __________
            Page No. __________   Line No. __________

            Divided by: ÷

        Average Month Total Expenses $ __________
            Page No. __________   Line No. __________

        Equals Months Supply of Cash

                                          ____
                                          MONTHS

II. RECEIVABLES

    A. SERVICE, PARTS, AND BODY SHOP

        1. Service, Parts, and Body Shop Receivables $ __________
            Page No. __________   Line No. __________

            Total Service, Parts,
                and Body Shop Sales YTD $ __________
            Page No. __________   Line No. __________
                   Less: (-)

        YTD Warranty and Internal Sales $ __________
            Page No. __________   Line No. __________

        Equals YTD Chargeable Sales $ __________

        Divide by 12 to obtain Average Month Chargeable Sales $ __________

    B. FINANCE AND INSURANCE COMPANY

        1. Finance and Insurance Co. Recievables $ __________
            Page No. __________   Line No. __________

        Finance and Insurance Co. Sales YTD $ __________   ÷
            Page No. __________   Line No. __________

        Divide by 12 to obtain Average Month Sales $ __________

        Divide Average Month Sales into F&I Recievables
        to obtain months supply of Recievables

                                          ____
                                          MONTHS

TOTAL DEALERSHIP CASH FLOW ANALYSIS

C.   WARRANTY

     1. Warranty Receivables $ ___________

Page No. __________   *Line No.* ____________

     YTD Warranty Sales $ __________   ÷

Page No. __________   *Line No.* ____________

     Divide by 12 to obtain Average Month Warranty Sales $ __________

     Divide by Average Month Sales into
Receivables to obtain Months Supply

____
MONTHS

III.   INVENTORIES

A.   DEMONSTRATORS

     1. Actual

Page No. __________   *Line No.* ____________

____

B.   NEW VEHICLES - UNITS

     1. Current End of Month Inventory Including Demos

Page No. __________   *Line No.* ____________

____
UNITS

     Current Month Sales - Retail $ __________   ÷
UNITS

Page No. __________   *Line No.* ____________

     Divide by Daily Sales Rate
(Sales Divided by Selling Days - 25)

____
UNITS

     Equals Days Supply (Inventory Divided by Daily Sales Rate)

____
D/S

TOTAL DEALERSHIP CASH FLOW ANALYSIS

C. **USED VEHICLES**

1. Current End of Month Inventory
   Page No. ___________ _Line No._ ___________
   ____
UNITS

   Current Month Sales - Retail
   Page No. ___________ _Line No._ ___________
   ___________ UNITS ÷

   Divide by Daily Sales Rate
   (Sales Divided by Selling Days - 25)
   ____
UNITS

   Equals Days Supply (Inventory Divided by Daily Sales Rate) ___________ D/S

D. **PARTS AND ACCESSORIES**

1. Current End of Month Inventory
   (or Average E.O.M. Inventory) $___________
   Page No. ___________ _Line No._ ___________

   YTD Cost of Sales $___________ ÷
   (Sales less Gross Profit)
   Page No. ___________ _Line No._ ___________

   Divided by Average Month Cost of Sales $___________
   (YTD Cost of Sales Divided by 12)

   Equals Months Supply of Parts ___________ M/S

E. **OTHER INVENTORIES**

1. Gas and Oil
   Page No. ___________ _Line No._ ___________

   A. Current End of Month Inventory $___________

   YTD Cost of Sales $___________ ÷
   (Sales less Gross Profit)
   Page No. ___________ _Line No._ ___________

   Divided by Average Month Cost of Sales $___________
   (YTD Cost of Sales Divided by 12)

   Equals Months Supply of Gas and Oil ___________ M/S

TOTAL DEALERSHIP CASH FLOW ANALYSIS

E.   OTHER INVENTORIES (continued)

    2. Paint and Body Shop Materials
        Page No. __________   Line No. ______________

    a. Current End of Month Inventory $__________

      YTD Cost of Sales $__________

      (Sales less Gross Profit)   ÷
        Page No. __________   Line No. ______________

      Divided by Average Month Cost of Sales $__________
      (YTD Cost of Sales Divided by 12)

      Equals Months Supply of Gas and Oil

                                       ____
                                            M/S

    3. Sublet Repairs

    a. Sublet Repairs Sales YTD $__________
        Page No. __________   Line No. ______________

      Divided by: ÷

    Divided by Labor Sales $__________

      Equals Percent Sublet Repairs of Labor Sales   __________%

IV.   OTHER CURRENT ASSETS

A. Prepaid Expenses % of Total Expense

    1. Prepaid Expenses $__________
        Page No. __________   Line No. ______________

                                        ÷

    Divided by Average Month Total Expenses $__________
    (YTD divided by 12)
        Page No. __________   Line No. ______________

      Equals Percent Sublet Repairs of Labor Sales   __________%

V.   FIXED ASSETS

A. Building and Leasehold

    1. Review Depreciation Schedule

B. Furniture, Fixtures, Sign

    1. Review Depreciation Schedule

C. Machinery and Equipment

    1. Review Depreciation Schedule

TOTAL DEALERSHIP CASH FLOW ANALYSIS

LIABILITIES

I. ACCOUNTS PAYABLE

A. Formula:

Accounts Payable $___________
  Page No. ___________   Line No. _____________

Divided by: ÷

Divided by Total Expenses (YTD divided by 12) $___________
  Page No. ___________   Line No. _____________

Equals Percent Accounts Payable of   ___________%
Average Monthly Expense

II. NOTES PAYABLE

A. Vehicles and Demos - Dealership Policy

1. Out of Trust - Notes Payable New Vehicles and Demos in excess of New
   Vehicle and Demo Inventory

2. Current Amount - Long Term Debt
   Current portion of Long Term Debt payable within
   12 months

B. Used Vehicles - An amount in this account is a "red light". Shortage
   of cash is indicated.

III. ACCRUED LIABILITIES
Any expenditure that is to be paid at a future date should be accrued each month.

A. Long Term Debt - Portion of principal usually paid each year
   with interest on unpaid balance.

TOTAL DEALERSHIP CASH FLOW ANALYSIS

NET WORTH

I.   COMMON STOCK
Original Investment

II.   RETAINED EARNINGS
Earnings from previous periods retained in business

III.   TOTAL NET WORTH

    A.   Composition

        1. Common Stock

        2. Retained Earnings

        3. Profit or Loss for the Period

    B.   Trend Analysis

        1. Net worth should be increasing each year. Comparisons to past periods will indicate the trend.

IV.   NET WORKING CAPITAL

    A.   Formula:

Current Assets $ ___________
Page No. ___________ *Line No.* ___________

Less sum of : (Current Liabilities plus
current amount of Long Term Debt) $ ___________
Page No. ___________ *Line No.* ___________

        Equals Net working Capital $ ___________

THE CASH FLOW SQUEEZE

INVENTORIES

NEW VEHICLES

$ _______ / Avg. Month Cost of Sales   X   1.5 (GUIDE)   = $ [Your Objective] $ _______ Actual   = $ _______ Cash Drain
Act. - Obj. X 1-Mo.
Floor Plan Interest Rate

USED VEHICLES

$ _______ / Avg. Month Cost of Sales   X   1.0 (GUIDE)   = $ [Your Objective] $ _______ Actual   = $ _______ Cash Drain *

PARTS INVENTORY

$ _______ / Avg. Month Cost of Sales   X   2.0 (GUIDE)   = $ [Your Objective] $ _______ Actual   = $ _______ Cash Drain *

RECEIVABLES

PARTS, SERVICE & BODY SHOP

$ _______ / Avgerage Month Chargable Sales   X   50% (GUIDE)   = $ [Your Objective] $ _______ Actual   = $ _______ Cash Drain *

PARTS, SERVICE & BODY SHOP

$ _______ / Current Receivables   X   10% (Past Due Guide)   = $ [Your Objective] $ _______ Actual Past Due   = $ _______ Cash Drain *

WARRANTY

$ _______ / Average Month Sales   X   0 **   = $ [Your Objective] $ _______ Actual   = $ _______ Cash Drain *

TOTAL CASH DRAIN (FROZEN CAPITAL) $ [   ]

* If Actual is less than Objective, enter "0" on Cash Drain Line
** "0" for Ford and GM, "1.0" for all others

CASH FLOW FORECAST

	THROUGH		
		MONTH	
CASH RECEIPTS			
VARIABLE & FIXED SALES			
OTHER INCOME & DEDUCTIONS (EXCLUDING			
FINANCE INCOME & ADJUSTMENTS FOR			
DOUBTFUL ACCOUNTS)			
NEW VEHICLE HOLDBACK			
SALES OF SECURITIES,			
FIXED AND OTHER ASSETS			
MISC. NOTES & ACCOUNTS RECEIVABLE			
TOTAL CASH RECEIPTS			
CASH DISBURSEMENTS			
NOTES PAYABLE - NEW VEHICLES & DEMOS			
NOTES PAYABLE - L&R UNITS			
DIRECT COST - L&R UNITS			
(EXCLUDING DEPRECATION)			
PURCHASES - P&A AND OTHER INVENTORIES			
VARIABLE SELLING EXPENSES			
COMPENSATION - TECHNICIANS			
TOTAL FIXED OVERHEAD EXPENSES			
(EXCLUDING PREPAID & ACCRUED ITEMS AND			
DEPRECIATION AND AMORTIZATION			
PREPAID AND ACCRUED EXPENSES			
BONUSES			
DIVIDENDS OR WITHDRAWALS			
PURCHASES OF SECURITIES,			
FIXED AND OTHER ASSETS			
INCOME TAXES			
PRINCIPAL PAYMENT ON NOTES			
OTHER THAN VEHICLES			
MISCELLANEOUS DISBURSEMENTS			
TOTAL CASH DISBURSEMENTS			
TOTAL CASH & CONTRACTS BEGIN OF PERIOD			
NET CASH FLOW			
TOTAL CASH CONTRACTS END OF PERIOD			

PROFIT CENTERING
(NEW VEHICLE DEPARTMENT)

I. COST OF SELLING A NEW VEHICLE

A. Formula:

YTD New Vehicle Variable Selling Expense .... $__________

Page No. __________ *Line No.* __________ +

Plus YTD New Vehicle Fixed Overhead .... $__________

Page No. __________ *Line No.* __________

Equals Total Expense New Vehicle Department .... $__________

Divided by: ÷

YTD New Vehicle Unit Sales .... __________
UNITS

Page No. __________ *Line No.* __________

Equals Average Cost of Selling a New Vehicle .... $__________

II. SALES MANAGER'S SALARY % OF NEW VEHICLE DEPT. GROSS

A. Formula:

YTD Salary - Supervision - New Vehicle Dept. .... $__________

Page No. __________ *Line No.* __________

Divided by: ÷

New Vehicle Dept. Gross Profit YTD .... $__________

Page No. __________ *Line No.* __________

Equals Salary % of Gross .... __________%

III. NEW UNIT SUPERVISION SALARIES

CURRENT MONTH		YEAR TO DATE
$__________	Salaries - Supervision - New Vehicle Dept.	$__________
	Page No. __________ *Line No.* __________	
÷	Divided by:	÷
__________	Number of New Units Sold	__________
	Page No. __________ *Line No.* __________	
$__________	Equals New Unit Supervision Salaries	$__________
	Per New Unit Sold	

PROFIT CENTERING (continued)
(NEW VEHICLE DEPARTMENT)

IV. SALESPERSON'S COMPENSATION % OF GROSS PROFIT

A. Formula:

Compensation - Vehicle Salesperson YTD $__________

Page No. __________   *Line No.* __________

Divided by: ÷

Gross Profit YTD $__________

Page No. __________   *Line No.* __________

Equals Compensation % of Gross Profit   __________%

V. SALESPERSON'S COMPENSATION PER NEW UNIT SOLD

CURRENT MONTH   YEAR TO DATE

$__________   Salespersons' Compensation - New Vehicle $__________

Page No. __________   *Line No.* __________

÷   Divided by: ÷

__________   Number of New Units Sold   __________

Page No. __________   *Line No.* __________   UNITS

$__________   Equals Salespersons' Compensation $__________

Per New Unit Sold

VI. SALESPERSON'S COMPENSATION PER NEW UNIT SOLD

A. Formula:

Advertising YTD $__________

Page No. __________   *Line No.* __________

Divided by: ÷

New Units Sold YTD   __________

Page No. __________   *Line No.* __________   UNITS

Equals Advertising Per New Vehicle Sold $__________

VII. DEMONSTRATOR EXPENSE PER NEW UNIT SOLD

    A.   Formula:

Demo Expense YTD $ __________
    Page No. __________   *Line No.* __________

    Divided by: $\div$

New Units Sold YTD
    Page No. __________   *Line No.* __________   UNITS

    Equals Demo Expense Per New Vehicle Sold $__________

VIII. F & I INCOME PER NEW VEHICLE SOLD

    A.   Formula:

F & I Income YTD New $ __________
    Page No. __________   *Line No.* __________

    Divided by: $\div$

New Units Sold YTD
    Page No. __________   *Line No.* __________   UNITS

    Equals F & I Income Per New Vehicle Sold $__________

IX. SALESPERSON PRODUCTIVITY AVERAGE SALES PER MONTH

    A.   Formula:

Total New and Used Unit Sales   __________
    Page No. __________   *Line No.* __________

    Divided by: $\div$

Number of Salespersons   __________
    Page No. __________   *Line No.* __________

Equals Average Units Sold per Salesperson YTD   __________

Divide by 12 Equals Average Per Month   __________

PROFIT CENTERING (continued)
(NEW VEHICLE DEPARTMENT)

X. NEW UNIT VARIABLE SELLING EXPENSES

CURRENT MONTH   YEAR TO DATE

$____________   New Unit Selling Expense $____________
Page No. ________   *Line No.* ________

÷   Divided by: ÷

____________   Number of New Units Sold   ____________
Page No. ________   *Line No.* ________   UNITS

$____________   Equals Variable Selling Expense $____________
                         Per New Unit Sold

XI. CUSTOMER RELATIONS ADJUSTMENTS/POLICY WORK PER NEW UNIT SOLD

A.   Formula:

Customer Relations Adjustments/Policy
Work - New Vehicles YTD $____________
Page No. ________   *Line No.* ________

Divided by: ÷

New Units Sold YTD   ____________
Page No. ________   *Line No.* ________   UNITS

Equals Policy Work Per New Vehicle Sold $____________

XII. LOCAL ADVERTISING - PER NEW VEHICLE RETAILED

A.   Formula:

Local Advertising YTD $____________
Page No. ________   *Line No.* ________

Divided by: ÷

New Vehicles Retailed YTD $____________
Page No. ________   *Line No.* ________

Equals Local Advertising - Percent of Sales
- New Vehicle Dept.   ____________%

XIII. DEPARTMENTAL GROSS PROFIT - PERCENT OF DEPARTMENTAL SALES

A. Formula:

New Vehicle Dept. Gross Profit YTD
(Including F & I) $__________
Page No. __________   *Line No.* __________

Divided by: ÷

New Vehicle Dept. Sales YTD $__________
Page No. __________   *Line No.* __________

Equals New Vehicle Dept. Gross
Profit % of Sales YTD   __________%

XIV. FLOOR PLAN INTEREST PER NEW UNIT SOLD

CURRENT MONTH   YEAR TO DATE

$__________   New Vehicle Dept. Floor Plan Interest $__________
                   Page No. __________   *Line No.* __________

   ÷   Divided by: ÷

__________   Number of New Units Sold   __________
                   Page No. __________   *Line No.* __________   UNITS

$__________   Equals Floor Plan Interest Expense $__________

                   Per New Unit Sold

**XV. DEPARTMENTAL OPERATING PROFIT OR LOSS - PERCENT
OF DEPARTMENTAL SALES**

A. Formula:

Department Profit or Loss - Dept. A YTD $__________
Page No. __________   *Line No.* __________

Divided by: ÷

New Vehicle Dept. Sales YTD $__________
Page No. __________   *Line No.* __________

Equals Departmental Profit or Loss - Percent
of Sales New Vehicle Dept. YTD   __________%

PROFIT CENTERING (continued)
(USED VEHICLE DEPARTMENT)

I. COST OF SELLING A USED VEHICLE

   A. Formula:

   Total Operating Expense U/V Dept. YTD $__________
   Page No. __________   *Line No.* __________

   Divided by: ÷

   Used Vehicle Units Sales Retail, YTD   __________
   Page No. __________   *Line No.* __________

   Equals Average Cost of Selling a Used Vehicle $__________

II. AVERAGE UNIT VALUE PER USED VEHICLE IN INVENTORY

   A. Formula:

   Dollar Inventory - Used Vehicles YTD $__________
   Page No. __________   *Line No.* __________

   Divided by: ÷

   Number of Used Vehicles in Inventory   __________
   Page No. __________   *Line No.* __________   UNITS

   Equals Average Unit Value per Used Vehicle
   in Inventory $__________

III. AVERAGE UNIT COST PER USED VEHICLE SOLD RETAIL

   A. Formula:

   Cost of Sales - Used Vehicles - Retail YTD (Sales - Gross) $__________
   Page No. __________   *Line No.* __________

   Used Vehicles - Retail - Reconditioning YTD $__________
   Page No. __________   *Line No.* __________

   Used Vehicles Adj. to Inventory YTD $__________
   Page No. __________   *Line No.* __________

   Equals Total Cost of Used Vehicles Sold Retail $__________

   Divided by: ÷

   Number of Used Vehicles Sold Retail YTD   __________
   Page No. __________   *Line No.* __________

   Equals Average Unit Cost
   Per Used Vehicle Sold Retail $__________

   Cost of Sales = Sales Less Gross Profit

IV.   AVERAGE UNIT VALUE PER USED VEHICLE SOLD WHOLESALE

A.   Formula:

Cost of Sales - Used Vehicles W/S   (Sales - Gross) $________

Page No. __________   Line No. ______________

Divided by: ÷

Number of Used Vehicles Sold W/S   ________
UNITS

Page No. __________   Line No. ______________

Equals Cost per Used Vehicle Sold W/S $________

V.   DEPARTMENTAL OPERATING PROFIT OR LOSS - PERCENT OF DEPARTMENTAL SALES

A.   Formula:

Department Profit or Loss - Dept. B - YTD $________

Page No. __________   Line No. ______________

Divided by: ÷

Used Vehicle Dept. - Total Sales YTD $________

Page No. __________   Line No. ______________

Equals Departmental Profit or Loss - Percent of Retail Sales   ________%

VI.   RETAIL GROSS PROFIT PER USED VEHICLE SOLD RETAIL

A.   Formula:

Gross Profit - Used Vehicles Sold Retail YTD $________

Page No. __________   Line No. ______________

Less:

Reconditioning Vehicle Retail YTD $________   (-)

Page No. __________   Line No. ______________

Adjustment - Used Vehicle Inventory YTD $________ $________

Page No. __________   Line No. ______________

Equals Adjusted Gross Profit - PUVR $________

Divided by: ÷

Number of Used Vehicles Sold Retail, YTD   ________

Page No. __________   Line No. ______________

Equals Gross Profit per Used Vehicle Sold Retail $________

VII. RECONDITIONING PER USED VEHICLE SOLD RETAIL

A. Formula:

Used Vehicles Retail - Reconditioning YTD $________

Page No. __________   *Line No.* ____________

    Divided by: ÷

Number of Used Vehicles Sold Retail YTD   ________

Page No. __________   *Line No.* ____________

Equals Reconditioning per Used Vehicle Sold Retail $________

VIII. DEPARTMENTAL GROSS PROFIT AS PERCENT OF DEPARTMENTAL SALES

A. Formula:

Used Vehicle Dept. Gross Profit YTD $________

Page No. __________   *Line No.* ____________

    Divided by: ÷

Used Vehicle Department - Sales, YTD $________

Page No. __________   *Line No.* ____________

Equals Used Vehicle Department Gross Profit
As Percent of Sales - Used Vehicle Dept.   ________%

IX. SELLING RATIO - USED RETAIL TO TOTAL USED

A. Formula:

Number of Used Units Sold at Retail, Total YTD   ________

Page No. __________   *Line No.* ____________

    Divided by: ÷

Number of Used Units Sold YTD   ________

Page No. __________   *Line No.* ____________

Equals Ratio of Used Retail to Total Used   ____ to ____

VARIABLE OPERATIONS

I. VARIABLE NET PROFIT PER NEW UNIT SOLD

CURRENT MONTH   YEAR TO DATE

$____________ Variable Gross Profit $____________

Page No. ____________ Line No. ____________

(Less)   (Less)

$____________ Total Variable Selling Expense $____________

Page No. ____________ Line No. ____________

$____________ Equals Variable Net Profit $____________

÷   Divided by: ÷

____________ Number of New Units Sold   ____________

$____________ Equals Variable Net Profit Per New Unit Sold $____________

II. VARIABLE NET OPERATION SUMMARY

Compute the following percentages of sales on each item as listed for the New Vehicle and Used Vehicle Departments. Carry out to tenths of percent.

	NEW VEHICLE		USED VEHICLE	
ITEM	MONTH	YTD	MONTH	YTD
SALES	100 %	100 %	100 %	100 %
COST OF SALES	_____ %	_____ %	_____ %	_____ %
OPERATING INCOME (GROSS PROFIT)	_____ %	_____ %	_____ %	_____ %
VARIABLE EXPENSES	_____ %	_____ %	_____ %	_____ %
PERSONNEL EXPENSES	_____ %	_____ %	_____ %	_____ %
SEMI-FIXED EXPENSES	_____ %	_____ %	_____ %	_____ %
FIXED EXPENSES	_____ %	_____ %	_____ %	_____ %
TOTAL EXPENSES	_____ %	_____ %	_____ %	_____ %
DEPARTMENT NET PROFIT (OR LOSS)	_____ %	_____ %	_____ %	_____ %

PROFIT CENTERING
(SERVICE DEPARTMENT)

I.   SERVICE DEPARTMENT EFFECTIVE LABOR RATES

A.

22	Work Days Per Month
X 8	Average Hours
176	Total Available Hours
X 90%	Productivity
158.4	Billable Clock Hours
X 130%	Efficiency
205.9	Flat Hours Available
X 5	Number of Technicians
1029.5	Flat Rate Hours (Customer Billing)

B.   Total Expense Service Department Average Month

Service Dept. = \$______________ ÷ 12 =   \$ ________
        Page No. __________   *Line No.* _____________

C.   Cost of Sales Service Department

YTD (Sales - Gross)   \$ ________
        Page No. __________   *Line No.* _____________

                                                          +

YTD (Sales - Gross)   \$ ________
        Page No. __________   *Line No.* _____________

                                                          = ________

Plus Adjustment Cost of Sales   + \$ ________
        Page No. __________   *Line No.* _____________

Equals Annual Cost of Sales   = \$ ________

Divided by 12 = Average per Month   \$ ________

D. $\dfrac{B + C}{A}$ Equals Effective Labor Rate Just to Break - Even

______________ + ___________ ÷ ______________ = \$ __________ Per Hour to
                                                              Break - Even

II. DEPARTMENTAL PROFIT OR LOSS - PERCENT OF DEPARTMENT SALES

  A. Formula:

Department Profit or Loss - Dept. C. YTD $__________
  Page No. __________   *Line No.* __________

  Divided by: ÷

Service Department Sales, YTD $__________
  Page No. __________   *Line No.* __________

Equals Departmental Profit or Loss
As Percent of Sales - Service Dept.   __________ %

III. FIXED ABSORPTION (FIXED COVERAGE OR SERVICE ABSORPTION)

  A. Formula:

$$\frac{\text{Fixed Gross Profit}}{\text{Fixed Overhead}}$$

Service Dept. Gross YTD $__________
  Page No. __________   *Line No.* __________

Plus   +

Parts and Access. Dept.
Gross YTD $__________
  Page No. __________   *Line No.* __________

Plus   +

Body Shop Dept. Gross YTD. $__________
  Page No. __________   *Line No.* __________

Equals Total Fixed Gross Profit $__________

                                                                 ÷

Total Fixed Overhead YTD $__________
  Page No. __________   *Line No.* __________

Equals Fixed Absorption   __________ %

IV. AVERAGE MONTH TIME DISTRIBUTION YEAR - TO - DATE

	SALES		LABOR RATE		FR HOURS GENERATED	PERCENT
Customer	__________	÷	__________	=	__________	______ %
Warranty	__________	÷	__________	=	__________	______ %
Internal	__________	÷	__________	=	__________	______ %
TOTAL	$__________		TOTAL HOURS	__________		100%

V. REPAIR ORDER ANALYSIS

$____________________ ÷ ________________ = $________________ .
YTD Sales   YTD Repair Orders   Sales per Repair Order
Page No. ______ *Line No.* ________

$____________________ ÷ ________________ = $________________ .
YTD Gross Profit   YTD Repair Orders   Gross per Repair Order

Page No. ______ *Line No.* ________

$____________________ ÷ ________________ = $________________ .
YTD Total Expenses   YTD Repair Orders   Cost to Write a
Service Dept.   Repair Order
Page No. ______ *Line No.* ________

$____________________ ÷ ________________ = $________________ .
Net Operating Profit   YTD Repair Orders   Net Operating Profit
Per Repair Order

Page No. ______ *Line No.* ________

$____________________ ÷ ________________ = $________________ .
YTD Prorated Administrative   YTD Repair Orders   Prorated Administrative
Expense   Expense Per Repair Order
Page No. ______ *Line No.* ________

VI. TECHNICIANS EVALUATION

$$\text{Average Productivity} = \frac{\underline{\text{Actual Hours Worked (Clocked)}}}{\text{Total Hours Available}} \qquad \underline{}$$
Guide

$$\text{Average Efficiency} = \frac{\underline{\text{Total Flat Hours Worked (Produced)}}}{\text{Actual Hours Worked (Clocked)}} \qquad \underline{}$$
Guide

$$\text{Flat Rate Hour Ratio} = \frac{\underline{\text{Total Flat Rate Hours (Produced)}}}{\text{Total Hours Available}} \qquad \underline{}$$
Guide

PROFIT CENTERING
(PARTS AND ACCESSORIES DEPARTMENT)

I. INVENTORY TURN (PARTS GROSS TURN)

A. Formula:

$$\frac{\text{YTD Net Costing of Sales}}{\text{Parts ending Inventory (or)}}$$
$$\text{Average Month End Inventories}$$

Net Sales YTD Parts & Access.		___________ $
Page No. __________ *Line No.* ____________		
Less Gross Profit.		___________ $
Page No. __________ *Line No.* ____________		
Equals Cost of Sales YTD		$__________
Divided by:		÷
YTD Ending Parts Inventory		$__________
Page No. __________ *Line No.* ____________		
Equals Annual Parts Inventory Turn		__________
		TIMES

II. PARTS ORDER PERFORMANCE

A. Formula:

Dollar Parts Purchased on Stock Orders	$__________
Divided by:	÷
Total Parts Purchased	$__________
Equal Parts Order Performance	__________ %

The data for this computation must be taken from the
Purchases Journal and Source Documents.

PROFIT CENTERING (continued)
(PARTS AND ACCESSORIES DEPARTMENT)

III. TRUE INVENTORY TURN
(TELLS YOU WHOSE INVENTORY YOU ARE TURNING)

    A. Formula:

Gross Inventory Turn
    (Times)   ______________ (Times)

Stock Order Performance   ______________%

Equal True Inventory Turn   ______________

Example: If Gross Turn is 4.0 and Stock Order Performance is 80% then True Turn is 3.2. This means you are turning the parts purchased on the stock order from the factory or distributor at an annual rate of 3.2 times!

IV. PERCENT RETURN ON PARTS INVENTORY

    A. Formula:

Net Operating Profit Parts Dept. YTD $______________
    Page No. ____________   *Line No.* ____________

    Divided by: $\div$

Parts Inventory
(Use Average Month Inventory when available) $______________
    Page No. ____________   *Line No.* ____________

Equals Percent Return on Inventory   ______________%

V. PARTS & ACCESSORIES SALES PER PARTS EMPLOYEE

    A. Formula:

YTD Average Month Parts & Accessories Sales $______________
    Page No. ____________   *Line No.* ____________

    Divided by: $\div$

Number of Parts Employees - Parts Dept.   ______________
    Page No. ____________   *Line No.* ____________

Equals Total Sales per Parts Employee $______________
    PER MONTH

PROFIT CENTERING (continued)
(PARTS AND ACCESSORIES DEPARTMENT)

VI. SOURCE OF PARTS SALES

	Sales	Percent of Total Sales

Parts on Repair Orders YTD
Page No. __________ *Line No.* ______________ $__________   __________ %

Warranty Claims YTD
Page No. __________ *Line No.* ______________ $__________   __________ %

Internal Parts Sales YTD
Page No. __________ *Line No.* ______________ $__________   __________ %

Counter Parts Sales
Page No. __________ *Line No.* ______________ $__________   __________ %

Wholesale Parts Sales
Page No. __________ *Line No.* ______________ $__________   __________ %

Accessories
Page No. __________ *Line No.* ______________ $__________   __________ %

TOTAL $__________   ___100___ %

PROFIT CENTERING
(BODY SHOP)

I. BODY SHOP SALES PER BODY SHOP EMPLOYEE

A. Formula:

Body Shop Sales Average Month
YTD Sales divided by 12 $______________
Page No. ____________ *Line No.* ______________

Divided by: ÷

Body Shop Employees Body Shop   ______________
Page No. ____________ *Line No.* ______________

Equals Body Shop Sales Per Employee $______________

II. BODY SHOP DOLLAR SOURCES OF LABOR SALES

	Sales	Percent
Customer Shop Labor YTD	$__________	__________ %
Warranty Claims YTD	$__________	__________ %
Internal Labor YTD	$__________	__________ %
TOTAL	$__________	___100___ %

Page No. ____________ *Line No.* ______________ (for each line above)

III.   REPAIR ORDER ANALYSIS

$_______________________   ÷   _______________   = $_________________ .
YTD Sales   YTD Repair Orders   Sales per Repair Order
Page No. _______ Line No. _________

$_______________________   ÷   _______________   = $_________________ .
YTD Gross Profit   YTD Repair Orders   Gross per Repair Order
Page No. _______ Line No. _________

$_______________________   ÷   _______________   = $_________________ .
YTD Total Expenses   YTD Repair Orders   Cost to Write a
(Body Shop)   Repair Order
Page No. _______ Line No. _________

$_______________________   ÷   _______________   = $_________________ .
Net Operating Profit   YTD Repair Orders   Net Operating Profit
                                                                                            Per Repair Order
Page No. _______ Line No. _________

$_______________________   ÷   _______________   = $_________________ .
YTD Prorated Administrative   YTD Repair Orders   Prorated Administrative
Expense   Expense Per Repair Order
Page No. _______ Line No. _________

FIXED OPERATIONS (continued)

I.   VARIABLE - FIXED MANAGEMENT

FIXED

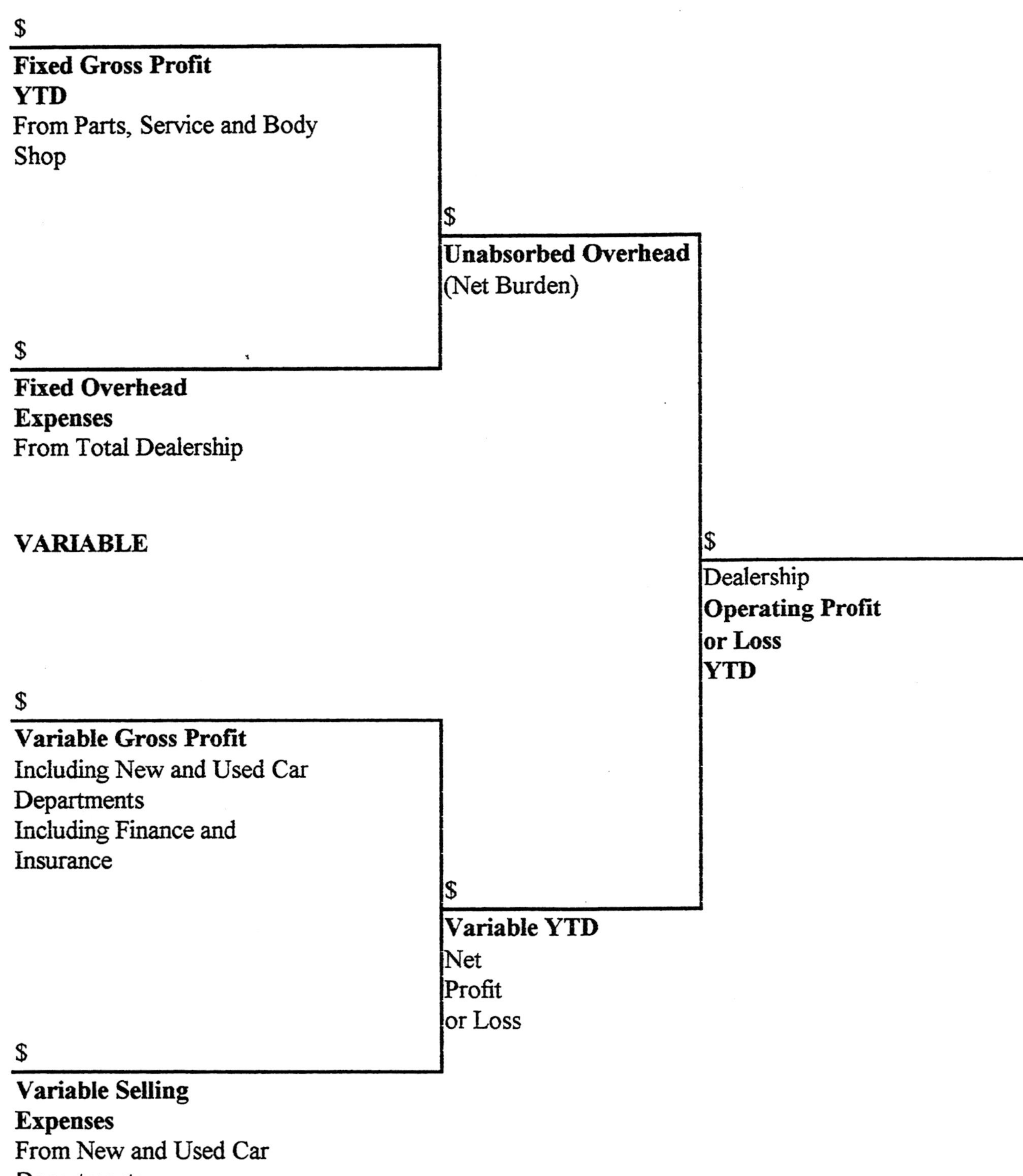

VARIABLE

GLOSSARY

DEALERSHIP BUSINESS MANAGEMENT GLOSSARY

Note: Does not include Lease and Rental

ABSORPTION See Fixed Coverage

ACCOUNTING DEPRECIATION The periodic reduction in the value of a fixed asset as it appears on the dealership balance sheet. The accounting depreciation rate is usually stated as a monthly percentage of original (acquisition) cost. Accounting Depreciation is also called "write-down".

ACCOUNTING PERIOD Time period for which financial statements which measure flows are prepared. Clearly identified on the financial statement.

ACCOUNTS PAYABLE Amount owed by dealership on an open account to a creditor for purchases of merchandise and services. A Current Liability.

ACCOUNTS RECEIVABLE Amounts owed to a dealership for the sales of goods and services made by the dealership on a charge (open) account. A Current Asset.

ACCRUAL BASIS OF ACCOUNTING The method of recognizing revenues as goods are sold (or delivered) and as services are rendered, independent of the time when cash is received. Expenses are recognized in the period when the related revenue is recognized independent of the time when cash is paid out.

ACCRUED LIABILITIES (one type of Current liabilities.) Obligations to pay, within 12 months of the date of the Balance Sheet, amounts for which the dealership has not yet been billed, but the obligations were incurred in the accounting periods prior to the date of the Balance Sheet.

ADDITIONS TO INCOME Monies or credits received by the dealership which are either not part of a departmental sale or income or not relevant to the Accounting Period of the statement. Typical items are interest earned, discount earned by prompt payment of Accounts Payable and Bad Debts Recovered (Accounts Receivable which were previously removed from inventory as uncollectible.)

ADJUSTMENT-COST OF LABOR SALES See Unapplied time.

ADMINISTRATIVE EXPENSE Expenses of a general or indirect nature; expenses which are not directly charged to one or more of the operating departments. Dealers often refer to these as "Z accounts."

APPRAISAL Process (usually utilizing an Appraisal Form) for determining the net value (estimated wholesale minus reconditioning) of a vehicle being offered to dealership for cash or in trade on another vehicle.

AREA OF PRIMARY RESPONSIBILITY The geographic area (communities) designated as "primary" for/to a dealership by a Division and employed in establishing the dealership's Planning Potential and making evaluations of the dealership's effectiveness.

ASSETS Items of value owned by the dealership. Assets are listed by classifications on the dealership Balance Sheet in their order of liquidity. Assets are classified as Current, Working, Fixed and Other. Current assets are the most liquid.

BALANCE SHEET A statement of financial condition (position) of the dealership as of a specific date.

BOOK VALUE See Net Book Value.

BREAK-EVEN UNIT (VEHICLE) Number of new vehicles sales (equivalencies) required to cover the Fixed Net Loss, adjusted in some accounting systems by Net Additions and Deductions to Income.

CAPITAL STANDARDS See Net Working Capital Standards

CARRY-OVER (CHANGE-OVER ALLOWANCE) See Close-Out Allowance

CHART OF ACCOUNTS The structural foundation of an accounting system, establishing the classifications under which transactions are reported. Vital as a guide to accounting uniformity and providing an organized system. Accounts are number coded as a memory aid and to facilitate machine accounting.

C.L.R.O. Customer Labor Repair Order

CLOSE-OUT (CARRY-OVER) Allowance An amount payable to deader by manufacturer (upon proper application) for each new and unused vehicle in deader inventory at time that vehicle model or designation is discontinued or replaced by another model or designation.

CONTRACTS IN TRANSIT The amount due the dealership from vehicle sale retail finance contracts which have been signed by the customer and submitted to finance institutions but for which dealership has not yet received funds.

COST OF SALES Total cost of goods and labor sold by a dealership in a specified accounting period. Cost of technician labor is the direct gross compensation exclusive of any benefits. Sales minus Cost of Sales equals Gross Profit.

CURRENT ASSETS Those assets which are cash or can be readily (less than one year of the Balance Sheet date) converted to cash. inventories of money, parts and accessories, new and used vehicles, accounts receivable and prepaid expenses are normally considered Current Assets. Current assets are carried in the accounting systematic acquisition cost or current value. They are the dealership's Gross Working Capital.

CURRENT LIABILITIES Amounts of money owed by the dealership and payable within 12 months of the date of the Balance Sheet. Trade accounts, taxes, insurance premiums and payroll are typical Current Liabilities.

CURTAILMENT Systematic reduction of the outstanding balance of a financial obligation.

CUSTOMER LABOR REPAIR ORDER (C.L.R.0.) Service Department work order wherein the major portion of the work to be performed will be paid for by a retail customer. Retail as contrasted to Wholesale, Internal or Warranty.

OPERATING CONTROL (D.O.C.) DAILY A report intended to keep dealership management informed as to their daily progress toward their sales, profit, expense and inventory goals. '

DAILY SALES RATE The average number of items sold per working day. Formula: month's total sales divided by number of working days in month.

DAYS' SUPPLY See Inventory - Days' Supply

DEDUCTIONS FROM INCOME Monies spent or not received as agreed which are not allocated to any particular department or not relevant to the Accounting Period of the statement. Deductions are such items as interest on loans and reserve to cover overage Accounts Receivable (adjustment for Doubtful Accounts Allowance).

DELAYED PAYMENT When referenced to Notes Payable-New Vehicles and Demonstrators, is the amount for which delayed payment privilege exists by Car/Truck Division agreement; one form of factor assistance for dealership fleet sales of vehicles.

DEPARTMENTAL PROFIT Excess of a department's gross profit over that department's expenses. May be before or after considering Pro-rated Administrative Expenses.

DEPRECIATION See Accounting Depreciation

D.O.C. Daily Operating Control

EFFICIENCY (TECHNICIAN) A measurement of the Technician's ability to perform a service operation within the time allowance in the Labor time Guide (Flat Rate) Manual.

FIFO - FIRST IN FIRST OUT Cost of sales is determined from oldest purchases in inventory. See LIFO.

FIXED ASSETS Relatively permanent assets owned by a dealership with these characteristics:

       a. Useful life to dealership longer than one year.
       b. Used in the operation of the dealership business.
       c. Not for sale during the planned useful life period.

Examples are buildings and equipment. Entered at acquisition cost. Also called Fixed Capital.

FIXED COVERAGE No industry standard. Proportion of Total Fixed Overhead Expenses covered by gross profits from sales of the Parts, Service (Mechanical and Body) Departments, i.e., the Fixed Gross divided by the Fixed Overhead. Usually expressed as percentage. Also called Absorption. N.A.D.A. published statistics are computed by converting all dealership ethyl to the GM format.

FIXED EXPENSES Those dealership expenses which remain almost unchanged from month to month. This is a sub-group of Total Fixed Overhead Expenses.

FIXED GROSS PROFIT Total Gross Profit of the Service (Mechanical and Body) and Parts and Accessories Departments.

FIXED NET LOSS Amount of Fixed Overhead Expenses not covered by Fixed Gross Profit. Fixed Overhead Expenses minus Fixed Gross Profit.

FIXED OPERATIONS Includes Mechanical and Body Service Departments and Parts & Accessories Department; those portions of the dealership less responsive to seasonal and economic fluctuations.

FIXED OVERHEAD (EXPENSES) All dealership expenses other than Variable Selling Expenses. Fixed Overhead is sub-divided into Personnel, Semi-Fixed and Fixed Expenses on many accounting systems.

FLAT RATE Price/cost/time relationship for services and repair work. Work operations are assigned a number of hours for which worker is paid and customer charged, regardless of elapsed time to perform work. Manufacturers publish Flat Rate (also called Labor Time Guides) for all regular mechanical and body repair operations.

FREE FLOOR PLAN Floor plan expenses or allowances paid by factory to dealership or dealership floor-planning source. Time period for free floor plan is part of the Selling Agreement and is usually a function of the holdback amount and payment schedule.

GROSS TURNS See Turnover Rate

INDIRECT EXPENSE Expenses of a general nature not directly applicable to an operating department. See Administrative Expense.

INTERNAL SALE Goods and services used internally by the dealership. Sometimes referred to as interdepartmental sales. These would appear as new vehicle predelivery expense, policy adjustment new and used vehicle, policy adjustment parts and service, used vehicle reconditioning, demo or company car expense.

INVENTORY ADJUSTMENT Accounting adjustment to inventory accounts to reflect changes in value caused by obsolescence, changes in market value or other variations between book and physical inventory. Usually applies to the inventory value of used vehicles, parts and accessories and labor (Work in Process).

INVENTORY BALANCE Makes, models, body styles, years of vehicles (new or used) in inventory as compared with sales; that is, not too many or too few of any classification. Balance depends on preferences of buyers and seasonal factors. It is a variable that is subject to constant change and needs watching. For new units, color, trim and option equipment must also be considered.

INVENTORY - DOLLAR DAYS' SUPPLY Similar to Units Days' Supply except calculated in dollar value for inventory and daily "cost of sales". Can be used to analyze inventories of used vehicles, parts, G.O.G., etc.

INVENTORY - UNITS DAYS' SUPPLY An estimate of the number of days it would take to sell current stock based on the current daily rate of unit sell. Calculated on a working-day-month as in this example: Average daily unit sales for last month (25 working days), 2 units. Present inventory, 30 units. Therefore, days' supply, in units, 15 days. See Turnover Rate.

INVENTORY TURNOVER See Turnover Rate

INVESTMENT TURNOVER RATIO The ratio of net sales to net worth. When period analyzed is less than 12 months, it should be annualized.

JOURNAL Book of original entry (into the accounting system) for recording transactions. A dealership standard accounting system will include numerous journals for each business month for sales, purchases, receipts, and disbursements.

LABOR RATE The hourly dollar rate charged by dealership for services performed by mechanical and body technicians. Usually varies by technician or operation skill level and type of operation (car/truck, internal/customer, mechanical/body). Is multiplied by Flat Rate (Labor) Time to determine labor charge for a service operation.

LABOR TIME GUIDE See Flat Rate

LEASEHOLD IMPROVEMENTS Permanent improvements, additions or renovation to facilities leased by a dealership and which, by law, become property of the facility owners. Balance of lease period usually determines the accounting depreciation rate used by dealership.

LEDGER The accounting book of final entry. There is a ledger (page/sheet) for each numbered account onto which are recorded to Debits and Credits to that account. The E.O.M. amount of each ledger is the amount in that account which ends up on the Balance Sheet or Operating Statement.

LIABILITIES What the business owes. Claims of outsiders. Divided into Current liabilities and Non-Current (Long-Term) liabilities.

LIFO - LAST IN FIRST OUT An inventory flow concept which, in times of inflation, can reduce profit and defer income taxes. See FIFO.

LONG TERM LIABILITIES Long term debt including mortgages payable and any accrued or deferred liabilities which are not to be paid out of current assets.

MONTHS' SUPPLY Length of time a given inventory will last at a specified monthly sales rate. Current dollars of inventory divided by average month's cost of sales. Often expressed using units in inventory and unit rate of sale.

NET BOOK VALUE Original cost of a Fixed or Working Asset less accumulated Accounting Depreciation up to the date of the Balance Sheet. Term "book" refers to the accounting records (bookkeeping).

NET SALES Sales exclusive of (net of) sales and use tax and after all returns, discounts and other allowances.

NET WORKING CAPITAL No industry standard. Excess of Current Assets, Working Assets, Accumulated LIFO Write-down and Qualified Long-Term Debt over liabilities excluding Mortgages Payable. Some manufacturers do not exclude the current portion of Long-Term Debt.

NET WORKING CAPITAL STANDARDS This is the dollar value of dealership's Net Working Capital determined necessary to sustain satisfactory operation of the dealership. Part of the contractual agreement between the dealership and manufacturer. Many manufacturers recompute the standard periodically.

NET WORTH What the dealership owns (Assets) in excess of what it owes (Liabilities). This, in other words, is the "book value" of the corporation. Also called Owners Equity; claims of insiders.

NUT (TWO DEFINITIONS) 1. The Total Overhead or total of all Expenses except Variable Selling Expenses. 2. Overhead in excess of Fixed Gross (the unabsorbed overhead).

OPERATING DEPARTMENT A dealership department which is treated as a profit center in the dealership accounting system; a department which makes sales, generates gross profit and is charged with all or a portion of certain expenses.

OPERATING PROFIT (OR LOSS) Total sales, less total cost of sales, less total expenses, but before the application of Additions to Income, Deductions from Income, bonuses and income taxes. This represents the profit derived directly from the normal operation of the dealership departments.

OTHER ASSETS Those assets consisting of certain receivables, items of an investment nature or other items of value which are owned by the dealership but which are usually not converted into cash in a short period of time and not used in the operation of the dealership.

OTHER DEDUCTIONS See Deductions From Income.

OTHER INCOME See Additions To Income.

OVERHEAD See Fixed Overhead Expenses.

OWNERS EQUITY See Net Worth.

PERCENT GROSS PROFIT The portion of the sale price which is Gross Profit. Divide the Gross Profits by related Sales account amount and convert to percentage.

PERCENT OF ABSORPTION See Fixed Coverage.

PERSONNEL EXPENSE (GROUP) Wages and benefit expenses for dealership employees. Excludes compensation paid to vehicle and F&I salespersons, and direct cost of service labor sales.

PLANNING POTENTIAL (P.P.) An annual new vehicle sales volume guide established by a manufacturer for a dealership location for use in planning minimum requirements for space needs, facilities, personnel and net working capital. Sometimes called Planning Volume (P.V.).

PNV Abbreviation for "Per New Vehicle (sold)".

PNVR Abbreviation for "Per New Vehicle Retailed".

POLICY ADJUSTMENT Method of reducing or eliminating the price paid by the customer or dealership department for goods and/or services received when such concession or price adjustment is not granted by contractual agreement (warrants) or as trade discount. Some standard accounting systems also carry a second account titled "Customer Goodwill").

POSTING Routine bookkeeping procedure of transferring the debit and credit amounts from Journals to the Ledgers.

PREPAID EXPENSES Expenses the dealership paid in advance of the actual consumption of the goods or service and which will be "expensed" as consumed. Examples are insurance, taxes, and advertising which are often paid at the beginning of the "paid for" period. A subgroup of Current Assets.

PRODUCTIVITY RATIO (TECHNICIAN) Relationship of the number of hours recorded on Repair Orders by the Technician divided by the number of hours the Technician is available for work as recorded on a time card. Normally stated as a percentage. Acceptable range is 82-92 percent.

PROFIT UNITS (VEHICLES) The number of new vehicle sales (equivalencies) in excess of the Break-even Unit.

QUALIFIED LONG-TERM DEBT (GM) Dealership capital borrowed from bona fide owner(s) of the dealership. To qualify, (with Contact Division) principal repayments during a period cannot exceed dealership profits for the period. In affect, QLTD does not reduce Net Working Capital.

RECOURSE Agreement between dealer and finance institution wherein under specified terms and conditions the dealer guarantees the net unpaid balance of a dealer-controlled retail finance contract which is in default.

RENT AND RENT EQUIVALENT Subgroup of dealership Fixed Expenses. Selected dealership occupancy costs and expenses. Includes amount written off as depreciation of facilities or improvements.

RENT FACTOR Cost of owning or leasing operating facilities per new vehicle delivered. Useful when preparing the Dealership Annual Business Plan or analyzing an operation. Total of Rent and Rent Equivalent divided by the new vehicle volume (planned or actual as applicable).

RETAINED EARNINGS After tax net income over the life of the dealership corporation less all income distribution (dividends).

RETURN ON INVESTMENT Ratio of pretax profit to investment. Expressed as a percentage for a given accounting period. Computed by dividing the pretax net profit for the period by the Net Worth at the start of that period. Should be annualized when computed for less than 12 months.

RETURN ON SALES Ratio of pretax profit to net sales. Expressed as a percentage for a given accounting period.

SALES SUMMARY Book of original entry used in some dealerships for high volume activities such as Mechanical Service Sales. The account totals on the Summary are transferred to a Journal.

SCHEDULE Supporting set of calculations which show how figures on a financial statement (or tax return) are derived.

SELLING EXPENSE See Variable Selling Expense.

SELLING RATIO (SALES RATIO) The ratio of used vehicle unit sales to new vehicle unit sales for a specified time period. May be   expressed to include all sales or may be limited to retail sales only.

SEMI-FIXED EXPENSE (GROUP) Operating expenses which vary with, but not in direct proportion to, sales volume. This is a sub-group of Total Overhead Expenses.

SERVICE ABSORPTION Term not recommended as it does not include any reference to Parts and Accessories. See Fixed Coverage.

STOCK ORDER ALLOWANCE Additional discount and/or other incentive offered by "the factory" to its dealers for placing parts orders in the amount, form, and/or manner prescribed.

STOCK ORDER PERFORMANCE See True Turns.

STRAIGHT-TIME OPERATION Irregular or unusual repair operation which is not included in Labor Time Guide, or the additional time required to perform a regular operation for reason(s) beyond control of the dealership.

SUBLET (REPAIR) Services or repairs performed on vehicles or vehicle subassemblies for the dealership when the dealership either is not equipped for the work, or is unable or unwilling to perform the work within the required time.

TAX SHELTER Legal reduction or postponement of income taxes. In this seminar used to mean tax deferring.

TRADING POLICY Dealership criteria for determining the acceptability of a vehicle retail sale. May include factors such as gross profit level, aftersale items, trade-ins, dealer-controlled financing and unit time in inventory.

TRAVEL RATE Annualized (or other specified period) vehicle sales based on sales rate or volume during a portion of that period.

TRUE TURNS (Parts inventory) See Turnover Rate. Turnover Rate times Stock Order Performance equals True Turns. Stock Order Performance is the ratio of dollars of parts purchased on Stock Orders to total parts purchases for the time period being analyzed: month, quarter or year.

TURNOVER RATE Number of times an inventory is (figuratively) changed or "turned" in a given period. Formula: Total number of items (or dollars at cost) handled during the period divided by average inventory during the period (at cost). The term can be applied to personnel, i.e., "Salesperson Turnover". In Parts Department this Gross Turns.

UNABSORBED OVERHEAD Same as Fixed Net Loss. Also called "nut".

UNAPPLIED TIME Amount paid to Mechanical Service and Body Service technicians which has not been accounted for as productive labor on repair orders, earned vacation time, or building or equipment maintenance. Might represent idle or lost time bud could indicate other problems or irregularities. Computed by subtracting the end-of-month Work in Process-Labor physical inventory from end-of-month Work in Process book inventory. Also called "Adjustment Cost of Labor Sales". Displayed on Operating Statement as an increase in cost of sale, decrease of Gross Profit and no sales. If computations produce an increase of Gross Profit, there is still a problem.

USED VEHICLE INVENTORY OVERAGED Used vehicles which have been in the dealership inventory over 30 days. Normally stated as a percentage of the total used vehicle inventors. Expressed in units and dollars.

VARIABLE EXPENSE See Variable Selling Expense.

VARIABLE GROSS PROFIT Generally, the combined gross profits of the New and Used Vehicle Departments, Lease and Rental Department and F&I income.

VARIABLE NET PROFIT The Variable Gross Profit less Variable Selling Expenses. Called Vehicle Sales Profit or Vehicle Net by some manufacturers.

VARIABLE NET PROFIT PER NEW VEHICLE SOLD Variable Net Profit divided by number of new vehicles sold. If divisor is retail sales only, then result is P.N.V.R.

VARIABLE OPERATIONS Vehicle sales, F&I and leasing operations of the dealership. Called "variable" because of volume (and profits) short-term sensitivity to seasonal and economic fluctuations.

VARIABLE SELLING EXPENSE (GROUP) Operating expenses which are directly related to vehicle sales and leasing and tend to vary in direct proportion to volume. Some Dealership Standard Accounting Systems include Vehicle Advertising and/or Floor Plan expenses in this expense group.

VEHICLE NET See Variable Net Profit.

VEHICLE SALES PROFIT See Variable Net Profit.